T Learning Guide Primary
S Classroom Management

Rob Barnes is a Senior Lecturer in Education at the University of East Anglia, Norwich UK. His interest in behaviour management began in his first teaching post in a tough docklands school, a trial by fire never to be forgotten. He has since supported teacher-trainees in their classrooms and, from the early 1980s, developed a particular interest in teaching the language of behaviour management.

Rob has taught art and design specialist courses and educational computing. His research interests have included formative assessment and study skills at degree level. Having originally studied at Hull College of Art as painter and print-maker, he regularly exhibits paintings and etchings mostly with an East-Anglian landscape theme. His other interests include orchestral playing and violin-making, for which he won a national prize for outstanding craftsmanship.

The Practical Guide To Primary Classroom Management

Rob Barnes

P·C·P

Paul Chapman
Publishing

First published 2006
Reprinted 2008

SAGE Publications Ltd
1 Oliver's Yard
55 City Road
London EC1Y 1SP

SAGE Publications Inc.
2455 Teller Road
Thousand Oaks, California 91320

SAGE Publications India Pvt Ltd
B 1/I 1 Mohan Cooperative Industrial Area
Mathura Road, New Delhi 110 044
India

SAGE Publications Asia-Pacific Pte Ltd
33 Pekin Street #02-01
Far East Square
Singapore 048763

British Library Cataloguing in Publication data

A catalogue record for this book is available
from the British Library

ISBN 978-1-4129-1939-5
ISBN 978-1-4129-1940-1 (pbk)

Library of Congress control number 2006901468

Typeset by C&M Digitals (P) Ltd., Chennai, India
Printed on paper from sustainable resources
Printed and bound in Great Britain by Cromwell Press Ltd, Trowbridge, Wiltshire

Contents

1   Aiming to be effective

He's only 12 years old and already excluded from three schools. He's surrounded by so many negative influences that the thought of him ever cooperating is a long way off. Unless, of course, we could change that. He needs to feel positive about something or whatever we do, it won't make much difference. The thing is that you just want someone to care about you, whatever you look like, however bright you are, or however many difficulties you might think you have.

(Headteacher)

Introduction

Whatever measures you take, punishments and systems you set up, rules you devise and strategies you have for gaining the upper hand, an unrewarding classroom ethos is going to prevent you from succeeding. No wonder managing a class of students is such a fine balancing act between enthusiasm and taking control of the situation. Ideally you would love it if students wanted to hang on your every word and not waste a second before settling down to work. The practical reality is that it takes skill and good management to achieve a buzz of enthusiastic activity in your classroom. The most effective of teachers achieve more by remaining rewarding to be with than by drifting into nagging, becoming a military dictator or sarcastic cynic. This takes some doing because teachers need to be firm and not tolerate bad behaviour, yet at the same time praise students, inspiring them to produce work of quality. Most beginners try to be positive, but sometimes they confuse this with being friendly and dishing out praise. They are surprised when children take advantage and try to undermine their ability to manage a class. If you have already experienced this, you will realize that skilled teachers have ways of doing things that are different from a beginner.

You may find when you teach that outwardly you are relaxed and in control, while inwardly at times your emotions are about to reach boiling point. When students try to test you, all genuinely positive comments can desert you just when they would be most effective. Rather than controlling student behaviour, it actually begins to control you. Your smiles begin to look more like sneers and the tone of your voice changes. This is exactly the moment to fall back on sound techniques and established classroom rules to survive. Otherwise you may feel that you are sitting on a keg of dynamite, just waiting for the explosion.

You will need a wide range of responses to students because quick-fix strategies do not exist. For example, imagine you are on your first teaching placement and a student you have never met before (let us call him Ross) comes in late and very slowly walks behind you as you are explaining something to the class. What do you do? How would you react if you knew that:

- Ross's favourite way to disrupt is to hit another child as he comes into the room and threaten to do worse if they tell their teacher;
- Ross has a reputation for being the class clown;
- Ross is a regular troublemaker who frequently tries to 'needle' teachers;
- the teacher has warned you not to stand any nonsense from this class, especially not from Ross;
- Ross has been asked to take a message around the school by the headteacher;
- Ross has Asperger's Syndrome (a form of autism); or
- Ross has Attention-Deficit Hyperactivity Disorder (ADHD)?

As you can see, the situation is not straightforward and I only know what I would do if I knew nothing about Ross. Other teachers would probably do something quite different. First, I would probably use as calm a voice as I could to demonstrate that I was not thrown by Ross's behaviour. I would speak to Ross long before he tried to perform at the front of the class. I would distract him and say: 'Good to see you here. Sorry, didn't catch your name?' Second, I would say 'Ross, find a seat as quick as you can so we can get on.' Finally, I would carry on with the lesson for a couple of minutes then check to see if Ross had responded. But what if Ross didn't find a seat? What if Ross was silent when I asked his name? You cannot make Ross find a seat however hard you try, so you may find that Ross continues to entertain himself and probably the class. If Ross didn't give me his name, I would ask another student. If he still didn't find a seat I would probably say, as calmly as I could, 'Ross, I can't make you find a seat, so we'll need to deal with this later. You'll need to explain.' I would probably smile at Ross and say 'If you want to join in, that would be good. Do the best you can.' If Ross continued to be difficult I would try to keep the rest of the class on side by saying 'Ross needs some help here, so we may need to ignore him for a while. We all have work to do.' Ross might join in or he might not, but as a teacher you cannot let Ross take over the class and it would be unwise to have a confrontation that Ross might win. Ross has a choice, which is to find a seat or explain himself later (Ross would probably find a seat as he does not know me).

No wonder teaching is stressful. I might feel angered by Ross but I know I need to remain outwardly calm. I might be tempted to shout at Ross, which would be the worst thing I could do. I do not know him yet, so instead of shouting I welcome him warmly. I behave as if I know exactly what I am doing. Most important of all, I firmly describe the behaviour that I want, not the behaviour that I do not. If that fails to work I let the class know what I want them to do (ignore Ross). I refer to the work and continue to demonstrate that I am in charge, not Ross. If I have scuppered his chance to take control he will probably have another go, but I will be ready for that.

Ross is not going to cooperate without some work on my relationship with him. Sometimes it is possible to capitalize on a student's interest.

> Connor was interested in rugby, so that was my way through with him. You get more from kids if you can run a club after school, or lunchtime. They need to see you in a different light and relate better. It's not every teacher who can talk about the local football team, but there's always something that catches their interest. I'd advise new teachers to get involved in out of school activities if they can . . . anything that helps them see you in a positive light. (Primary school teacher)

Ten principles of behaviour management

The ideas in this book are very practical, but will need to be adapted for the age group that you are teaching. Teachers usually adapt to the age range that they are teaching by slight changes to voice tone and phrasing. The suggestions in this book will need to be read with this in mind. Younger children, for example, do not respond well to a tough 'bite your head off' voice tone – they are more likely to burst into tears. Children who are older need to be spoken to in adult tones. Some teachers would say that all students should be spoken to like that, but you will make up your own mind. The structure of the chapters that follow is that each takes a different slant on behaviour management, expanding on some basic principles of class management.

Difficult students in a class misbehave for a number of reasons. Top of the list is wanting to feel important and be noticed. Even if they hit another student it is their way of feeling important and powerful. If they shout out, make noises and act as the class clown it is still a way of feeling important. Bad behaviour is often a cover-up for failing at schoolwork, but this is not always the case. Some students simply dislike being told what to do by anybody, whoever it may be. They bring with them a negative pattern from childhood that persists whenever they are asked to do something. Others find it much more fun to be disruptive than to do any work. These are the opportunists looking for ways to 'torpedo' sessions and opt out of having to make the effort to learn. Like students who bully others 'for a laugh', their personal agenda is one that includes having some influence. The idea that they should consider anyone else but themselves does not occur to them.

Since you cannot cure all these ills in the short term, there has to be some way to manage classroom behaviour. Most problems will never arise if students are involved and interested, but as a beginner you will find it hard to motivate some students who resist this.

Ten principles

1　Take centre stage in the classroom, sounding confident and in charge even if you do not feel that you are.
2　Give plenty of praise and encouragement without inadvertently labelling students as 'brilliant', 'clever', 'thick' or 'stupid'.
3　Avoid shouting and nagging. This is not effective, especially with very young children.
4　Avoid confrontation or an argument that you will likely lose.
5　When in doubt, always refer to the work and to any systems and habits that you expect from the class.
6　Give a difficult student the choice of doing something now or facing unspecified consequences later.
7　Keep the class on your side, even if you ignore a difficult child.
8　Avoid being so vigilant about minor incidents that you become a repressive and unrewarding teacher.
9　Keep up the pace and focus attention on the positive objectives of your teaching session, or students will find ways to disrupt.
10　Always describe the behaviour that you want ('Ross, I need you to...') rather than the behaviour that you are trying to stop ('Ross, stop doing that').

Remember that behaviour management is not an end in itself. It is a way of ensuring that work can be done effectively. Disruptive students are more often won over than controlled, so concentrating on the work, rather than the behaviour, will provide plenty of chances to praise them. As a teacher, you have the power to change what happens. You may not think so sometimes, but you do. These 10 principles will be explained throughout this book, but their success depends on your ability to create a good working relationship with your class. Making a class feel special and giving them a sense of achievement keeps them on your side, with the majority cooperating. This is rarely a matter of telling them how well they have behaved unless it is something specific, such as 'I was really impressed by how politely you said that', or 'Waiting your turn shows how grown-up you can be.' How well students work, and how well they learn, are far more lasting motivators than praise for behaving well. You are there to move them forward in their learning. They need to behave well without their behaviour becoming the main focus of the classroom.

The seventh principle listed has been explained already when dealing with Ross. The class was told to ignore him so that the teaching could continue.

Most classes would cooperate in ignoring Ross, unless he already has a gang of conspirators on his side. The strongest force in any classroom is often peer-group pressure to conform, so this can be used to advantage. Teachers can:

- create a culture that is characterized by 'Our classroom . . .' and 'We are learning . . .';
- avoid 'My classroom . . .' and 'You are learning . . .';
- be in charge of a class without losing sight of learning as a shared activity.

The first visit to a school

When you arrive at a school for the very first time, children will be naturally curious about you. This is true however experienced you may be, although by the time that you are a newly-qualified teacher you will have learned what to expect. Even if you want to appear confident it is usual to feel quite the opposite. If you have been invited to the school as a trainee to observe, there are still ways to make a good impression rather than be like a cardboard cut-out. Few teachers are going to take you aside and tell you what to do, so try to involve yourself from the start. Offer to help teachers and start talking with students, showing a genuine interest in their work. If you are a real beginner, talk to teachers concerning your observations about teaching and ask in particular what they do with a new class in September. They may not remember that they have a share in setting your programme, but you are likely to want to ask about how lessons start and finish, how teachers get attention and how they keep things going. Be ready for experienced teachers' notorious 'gallows' humour, as they gently tease you about the stresses of teaching.

Before you arrive at the school, be clear about what you are meant to do. Beginners may think they are there only to observe, but this does not mean hovering silently in classrooms and corridors. Headteachers vary in their preferences, but I have met many who were impressed by the fact that a trainee said 'Good morning'. Introduce yourself before you are asked what you are doing on the premises. Ask questions, but pick your moment. A busy teacher or headteacher does not want to hear your stream of consciousness or a description of your journey to the school. You will need to find out where equipment is kept, how the school behaviour policy works and what the classroom rules are. It is also worth arriving with something you could do with students, such as reading a story, if the teacher is called away for a few minutes. No teacher wants a passive trainee whose idea of action is to be like a vacuum cleaner sucking up information. Rather than hover over individual students, divide yourself between writing things down and talking with your students.

You do not want to stop children working, but you still need to establish a presence in the classroom by being involved. If you fail to establish a presence you will become like wallpaper. Sooner or later comes the moment for your very first conversation with your students. Some of them will be wary of you and some ready to try out their brand of minor cheekiness to see what you will do. This can be one of the most difficult moments because you probably want to be liked, yet have heard that it may be wiser not to smile until Easter. On your first visit, keep most of the conversation with students to the topic of their work because it is a relatively safe area of discussion. Show enthusiasm for what students are doing, but deflect personal questions as best you can by referring to work. Questions such as 'Are you here to find a new boyfriend?', and 'Are those your own teeth?' could be dealt with by using humour, but you might prefer to play safe with a work comment such as: 'We're here to work, not ask those kind of questions.' Your main aim is to become used to sounding professional as opposed to behaving like an older brother or sister. It will be some time before you can pitch this exactly right, so it is far better at this early stage to err on the side of caution. You will look and sound like a teacher if you do what teachers frequently do. Teachers spend most of their day talking about schoolwork and students expect them to do just that.

When later you take over the class without the teacher present, students will end their honeymoon period of compliance. Be ready to take swift action to make it clear that you are a professional who expects high standards and is quick to extinguish attempts to make stupid noises or ask silly personal questions. Your best bet for doing this is to remain calm and consistently follow class rules and routines if you know them. Make remarks such as 'We don't need *any* stupid noises', if you hear them and divert students by saying things such as 'Let's look at the diagram on the whiteboard.' Alternate between control statements such as 'I expect politeness and concentration' and work statements such as 'Hands up – who can tell me . . .?' When you feel more confident, you can joke with students. Experienced teachers can get away with all sorts of remarks which for you might cause uproar. Give yourself time to adjust but do take any opportunity to see the funny side of life (your science demonstration going wrong, making errors on the whiteboard, using a marker to write and finding it has gone dry).

Questions to leave out and statements to leave in

You are likely to learn the hard way which questions elicit the best response and which are definitely not in the script. A beginner might say, 'Would you like to get your books out please?', to which the answer could very well be 'No thanks. I'd rather read this comic.' 'Bethany. Are you sitting properly?' is not asking for an anatomical description, but it is a question inviting trouble. Bethany might agree to sit properly, but you have left open the chance that she could shrug her shoulders and say 'Why should I?'

A question such as 'Who's ready?' might be used by an experienced teacher because the class knows it means that they need to stop what they are doing and pay attention. A beginner may not have established enough presence to try questions such as these:

- Would you like to get your books out? (No, not really!)
- Are we all ready? (invites a chorus of Yeh! No!)
- Can you sit properly? (No! Yes! Probably!)
- Would you like to sit somewhere else? (No!)
- Who would like to do this? (Me! Me! Me! Me!)
- Can you make less noise? (No!)

Turning questions into statements of need is more effective. 'Bethany. Sitting properly please' is not optional. 'We need more concentration and less noise please' is quite different from 'Can you make less noise?'

A complete contrast to a rhetorical question is to say something that is a fully-loaded directive. For example, a rhetorical question might be: 'Would you like to sit on the carpeted area?', but a fully-loaded directive would be: 'I need you to think of a question to ask when you quietly come over to sit on the carpet.' This brief directive has stated a need, asked students to think and included the adverb 'quietly' when they were told where to sit. There are variations on this theme.

Using statements rather than questions

'Be thinking of a question about this when you quietly go back to your seats.'
'Think of what you need to do to be ready to sit on the carpet.'
'I'll be asking questions, so think about what you've just heard as you quietly make a start.'
'I'm looking for a quality start, so think about this work with mouths closed.'
'Maximum concentration on silent footsteps before you move quietly to the carpet.'

Whenever you use a statement, you retain the power in the situation. Classes quickly recognize a rhetorical question because experienced teachers do not use them – or if they do, the class knows better than to shout in chorus. You also begin to demonstrate that you know what you want. Part of the process of becoming a teacher is learning to sound as if you are in charge, even if you do not feel like you are.

Demonstrating that you are in charge of the class

The main change during your early experience of teaching is from a stage where you respond to students' behaviour to a point where you take the initiative more strongly. You become better at spotting attempts to 'torpedo' your session and quickly involve students in the work despite themselves. Most likely the pace of your sessions will improve and you will understand how not to be sucked into students' every possible request. You cannot do this at first because it takes time to discover the many ways in which students say and do things. They can sound friendly, for example, when really they are being cheeky and trying you out. You may not know the difference when you first begin teaching so need to play safe and concentrate on your teaching. Demonstrating that you are in charge is not difficult so long as you stick to your intentions and know what you want to achieve. If you refuse to be deflected, you demonstrate that you are in charge. Do you want to be deflected when you are trying to explain a task? Do you want to be deflected when you are getting full attention from your class? Do you want to be deflected when you are trying to check that everyone has started the task?

There are important moments when students begin a task and you are intent on achieving a good start. If you are new to teaching, making a good start can take time to perfect because some students are brilliant at trying to divert your attention. You want to respond and help them, but if you do sometimes they will take you a step further away from what you are trying to achieve. One of the first things to learn about behaviour management is to resist being diverted by well-meaning interruptions, otherwise you cannot stick to the plot. There is a time and place for interactive teaching with lots of questions from children, but this may not be it.

Staying in charge by not overreacting

Nothing delights a disruptive student more than seeing that they have rattled you and therefore won a personal battle. Some students delight in finding creative ways to irritate a new teacher. When you are new to teaching you will find that they do this in assorted ways, including all manner of low-level annoyances. For example, a school policy may be to allow baseball caps in summer to shade against sunburn. After break a boy arrives in your classroom still wearing his cap, takes it off, sits down, then puts it on again – backwards. He slouches down under the desk and drums his fingers in anticipation. This is not the end of the world, but it is a silent challenge. The school policy is that caps are not worn in the classroom, so what do you do? You are a new teacher, so is this the first in a series of disruptive actions gradually escalating until you snap? Will this boy shout out a question or click his fingers to get your attention? Will he walk around the room when he is supposed to sit down and work? Will he try to make the class laugh with a smart remark? Will he mutter 'This is stupid' under his breath and be determined to do as little as he can? Will he invent one excuse after another about not being able to do the work? Will he sulk if you tell him off? Will he scowl and shout? Will he stack three chairs at the back of the classroom and sit on top of them, higher than his classmates? I have seen challenging students do all of these things. Unless you take action early, small disruptions become more ambitious ones. An experienced teacher would smile, use a matter-of-fact tone of voice and say 'Great hat Liam, but take it off so we can start please', or 'Sitting on one chair Darren, then we can start' then turn away, ignoring the students. Teachers will tell you not to overreact to bad behaviour simply because it will escalate the situation unnecessarily. Also, they may tell you to ignore some bad behaviour because responding to it is exactly what a badly-behaved student wants. Yet if you ignore bad behaviour, it can lead to more seriously bad behaviour, so what do you do? Ideally, you want badly-behaved students to learn that it is getting them nowhere. It certainly cannot be rewarded and there should be consequences that are uncomfortable for perpetrators. The most difficult decision you have to make as a beginner is how to respond without overreacting.

Staying in charge

A class of seven-year-olds is just settling down to do a written task. Some are about to use a computer and others will write about a science experiment. The activities have been explained and the students have had a minute or two to gather their equipment and begin. Two students immediately stick their hands in the air and shout 'Miss! Miss! Miss!' to demand their teacher's attention. Another tries to borrow a pen from a classmate. At this point their teacher has a number of options. She could ignore them. She could go over to them and see what they wanted. She could remonstrate because they are calling out, or she could take control of the situation another way. If she ignores them, she would not demonstrate that she is in charge. If they summon her to sort out their problems, she would still not demonstrate that she is in charge.

What this teacher actually did was to stand still, and say 'Just a moment, I'm checking *first* to see if everyone has started. Then I'll think about what you want.' She paused and checked again, adding 'I can see Kirsty has started. Well done Simon, Justin and Dylan.' Only when she was sure that the class had begun their work did she go over to the demanding students and respond to their apparent need. Other teachers will describe this teacher's strategy as 'sticking to the plot', 'being focused' or 'keeping your eye on the ball'.

Avoiding confrontation

Confrontation is more likely if you watch a student doing what you have just asked (remove a hat, sit properly, put something away). It is far better to behave as if the student has done what you asked already. Physically turn away and withdraw eye-contact. This is a key move in the art of not overreacting. The aim is not to escalate a minor problem into a bigger one. You need to be ready for attempts to draw you in, such as the student saying 'I'm not doing anything! Why pick on me?' Remain polite unless there is misbehaviour going on that simply cannot be ignored. Say what you want the student to do and quickly move on to something else.

Overreacting is signalled by agitated voice tone, gesture and action. Some teachers deliberately avoid this by adopting an approach which shows two contrasts of emotion in their voice: one is for negative comments, the other for positive ones. They save their emotional energy and enthusiastic tone for the positive and keep a very flat, dull, almost emotion-free voice for negative comments. The voice tone is as flat as they can manage. They sound as if they are reading a telephone directory. A practical example would be where they might say almost to themselves (without emotion and loud enough to be heard) 'That's not really getting us anywhere Dylan' and quickly find something to praise enthusiastically elsewhere in the room. Their voice rises and is energetic when giving praise. What they have done is to signal that they registered Dylan's bad behaviour, but were not going to be sucked in by it. The same flat tone of voice can be used to say 'Dylan, that's one minute of break time you just lost' or 'That's a pity, because you've chosen to repeat this work to correct it'. The 'telephone directory' voice is not a bored one – weariness and boredom transmit the wrong messages. Your voice needs to be purposeful and loud enough to be heard, but have no hint of wound-up frustration. You are assertive and purposeful because that will not reward bad behaviour.

The best classroom management occurs where your students are self-disciplined so that you do not need to control their behaviour. You will find this a useful longer-term management goal. Strategies for encouraging self-discipline are to be found particularly in Chapters 3 and 4 where some of the differences are explained between the rules that you impose and the codes of conduct that students can own for themselves. One of the anomalies of teaching is that you need to manage your class yet encourage them to develop the social skills to do most of the managing without you. You want to be less of a controller and more like a successful mentor. A beginner will find that this is way down the list of their personal expectations; even experienced teachers will tell you that it is a combination of inspired teaching and many hours of positive work when meeting a new class.

Turning misbehaviour to your advantage

Imagine a student, Luke, has just teased Kirsty and aggressively grabbed the available science equipment. An experienced teacher might smile, even laugh, but next deliver Luke a devastating 40 seconds of carefully honed crime prevention script. What begins as a smile gradually turns serious as the well-honed response rolls out. Eye-contact is compulsory. An observer would probably notice that as the speech continues, the teacher's voice becomes lower in pitch and aims for a certain uncomfortable confident gravitas. (Examples of scripts are given in Chapter 3.) The voice tone is pleasant at first, then changes to an emotion-free tone, taking on death-like qualities of shame and practised gravitas. There are awkward pauses within the gravitas, as descriptions of expected politeness, acceptable behaviour and consideration for others are reiterated. Eye-contact is like a laser beam (always there if the student looks at the teacher).

(Continued)

The psychology of this is first, to smile because this is unexpected. Second, to follow with whatever you can hone as a lengthy speech about what you really need from the student. As calmly as you can, deliver list upon list of what you want that seems to be missing, referring to the detailed importance of the work schedule, politeness, sharing and consideration *now*. Allow no interruption, as in 'No! I'm talking, you're listening', but drop in impossible questions such as 'What would happen if everyone grabbed the equipment?' Pause. Your 'speechifying' will false-foot misbehaviour just when the student thought it was safe to continue disrupting. End abruptly with a return to work and the threat of unknown consequences if there is further trouble.

So far, 10 principles of behaviour management have been introduced and a strong link has been made between demonstrating that you are in charge yet not overreacting to bad behaviour. This does not mean that you ignore bad behaviour but that you act appropriately as a professional teacher. You can take strong action without losing your cool. The following chapters show you ways to do this, enjoy your teaching and win the respect and friendship of your students. Techniques to gain the attention of a class, sustain a good start and deal with difficult students are explained, as well as the ways to prevent problems arising, deal with blank refusal and refuse to be hooked in by students who want to 'torpedo' your lessons.

Questions and issues for reflection

- What is meant by a good working relationship?
- How do I tell the difference between being cheeky and being friendly?
- How easy is it for teachers to be diverted by the demands of a few demanding students?
- What do I need to decide before I visit a school for the first time?
- What happens if teachers overreact to bad behaviour?
- What social skills do I definitely want to encourage in my children?
- When I intervene, am I creating difficulties or minimizing them?
- Am I able to treat children with respect, yet still let them know that there are consequences for poor behaviour?

Checklist summary

- A negative and unrewarding classroom ethos is going to prevent you from succeeding.
- Disruptive students are more often won over than controlled.
- Remember that as a teacher, you have power.

- Avoid rhetorical questions.
- The best classroom management occurs where your students are self-disciplined so that you do not need to control their behaviour.
- One of the first things to learn about behaviour management is to resist being diverted by well-meaning interruptions.
- Refusing to overreact keeps you in charge of the situation.
- You need to demonstrate that you are in charge.

Learning to keep your cool

Oh dear. You haven't even started your career and you're already joining the ranks of the perfectionists. One day you could be a headteacher, lying awake all night clutching a bottle of vodka, because you made a tiny error the day before.

(Ted Wragg, *Times Educational Supplement,*
18 November 2005)

Panic and perfectionism

The teaching profession is one where you can easily become a victim of perfectionism. Read any of the National Curriculum and standards for teaching and it all looks like a blueprint for a perfect education. Up and down the country there are teachers doing their best to teach as well as they can, most of them striving to do better. The sensible ones recognize that not every pupil can be interested all the time and not every lesson can grab the attention of bored students. During an average week in front of your class, you might teach one or two brilliant lessons and some that will be fairly good ones. The rest can frustrate you because they do not go as well as you would like. Some trainees and newly-qualified teachers worry mightily if they make the slightest mistake or panic if their students look bored. After a few successful lessons, they crank up expectations that lessons *should* be brilliant all the time, and students *should not* be bored.

The classic 'should' has its roots in an irrational belief that perfection is possible. When you work with children, not everything is within your control. A good deal of it is, but many students arrive in your classroom already overloaded with a number of difficulties which are not of your making. Some may have a disturbed and difficult background, or have had a late night. Others simply dislike any form of authority and do not want to be told what to do by you or anyone else. Some students want to talk, and some want to be left alone to get on with things by themselves. Some arrive already bored and listless.

There are also students who do not have much tenacity and want to get through their day with as little effort as possible. They may like you as a person, but that does not mean that they want to work hard. Occasionally the entire class will arrive and behave like a box of flies, agitated and almost impossible to calm down.

None of this is difficult to believe. The difficult part is understanding just how easy it is to click into a negative perfectionist mode without realizing. The signs are familiar as a dialogue chatters inside your head or is unloaded onto the nearest colleague:

- concentrating on what went wrong long enough to eradicate what went well;
- saying what went well, then adding a negative criticism beginning with 'but';
- feeling a failure if one or two students do not do as you want;
- feeling a failure because a lesson went really badly this time;
- unrealistically thinking that all your high standards can be met all the time;
- using the word 'should' and 'should not' a great deal;
- using absolute phrases such as 'complete disaster', 'never' and 'always';
- forgetting that it is normal for something to go wrong.

Such inner feelings of failure, anger, sadness or upset persist only if you feed them further with a dialogue of criticism. Sometimes it is a miracle that students do anything that teachers want them to do at all. You have a great deal of power in a classroom, but for various reasons your students agree to cooperate or not. Any teacher who tries to interest a class of children does this to see if they will respond and agree to learn something. Most students do, but not all students want to play this great game of life so you will be left with a few who have their own agenda. You can do your best for every student in your class, but it still takes two to learn. Monitor what your students achieve. Monitor how well you organize your teaching but leave aside the negative 'self-talk' or you will have a short career in teaching. Some things can be improved and put right, but there is plenty that is outside your control. There is a world of difference between wanting to teach well and wanting lessons to be brilliant.

How beginners can take 'centre stage'

Imagine what it can be like to stand in front of a class for the first time. Your stomach may feel as if it is somewhere round your neck and your feet are on a tightrope. Meanwhile you are trying to give an impression of confidence and calm. All this on top of the fact that so far, you have not taken charge of anything, only observed the class and helped a few students. You have been a classroom helper, not a real teacher. Students will have formed some impression already of who you are and how you can be approached. You are not likely to face your class without the class teacher being there, so there can be the added pressure of being watched as you take your first class.

Taking centre stage

- Move to a prominent position in the room and stand still with both feet glued to the ground. This needs to be with your back to a wall, typically at the front of the class.
- Tense the outer wall of your stomach slightly as if someone was about to punch you there. It is surprising how slack those outer muscles can go when you are nervous, leaving the inner ones to have their own private party.
- Feel a positive energy coming from the region of your stomach, outwards to the class, radiating warmth and confidence.
- Lower the pitch of your voice but not its volume. If you are anxious, you are likely to raise the pitch to a squeaky level and possibly speak too quietly. When you have gained attention, smile and lower the volume of your voice.

When you take centre stage this is not going to be in the centre of the room because you cannot see enough of the class. You need to provide a fixed focal point, not a confusing one where you explain things while walking round the room, or shuffling from one foot to the other. Students are not going to take much notice of things said as you move about. Feel your feet rooted to the spot and make sure your weight is on both feet. When we are apprehensive we tend to stand with our weight on one foot, probably with the other one ready to run out of the room. (You may need to ask students to move so that you can see them too.) Loss of volume and voice tone can transmit a low expectation that students will do what you ask. You are not talking to a close friend, so keep the voice as businesslike as you can. If ever you are in doubt, slow down, lower the pitch and keep the volume just loud enough for everyone in the class to hear you.

There is no such thing as one way to take centre stage. Some beginners are naturally reserved and others extrovert, but this is by no means any indication of how they will be in a classroom. I have seen shy beginners come alive with children and confident extroverts become very nervous indeed. What is certain is that in taking centre stage, you will need to have a much more public presence than usual. Anyone coming into your classroom should hear you using a public voice and not private whispers to individual students. This is not an excuse to shout, as that would send out the wrong signal. Aim your voice initially to reach the furthest wall from you if you are trying to get the class's attention especially if you are teaching PE or taking a class assembly in the school hall.

In addition, centre stage can be established by being fussy about the physical position of students in the classroom. Teachers who use the device of making sure that everyone can see will quietly move students into view or move them back if they are too near. Left to their own devices, students will often crowd too close or form groups not fully in the teacher's line of sight. For example, young children who are sitting round a table will try often to crawl to the centre or crowd you. Whenever you pause to organize the students or yourself, you are affirming your centre-stage presence in the classroom. There are plenty of excuses to do this because so much of teaching involves showing students how to use equipment or holding up examples. You also maintain your presence by pausing when students least expect it.

Sustaining your classroom presence

If you are working closely with an individual child, or a small group, pause and deliberately call across the room to a distant student. This has two consequences. It teaches the distant student that you are still in contact even though you are working with an individual. It also shows the individual student that you are going to make them wait long enough to check that other students are still working. When you move on to another student, they have got the message that you are always aware of what else is going on.

You can form a good habit if you take up your central position in the same way each time. Look as if you are trying to gain attention by remaining still, but also look as if you are pleased to start the lesson. A grim aggressive face as you scan the room is counterproductive to your aim of creating a good positive work atmosphere. If you look as if you do not expect to get attention (probably by frowning at the noise going on) you may invite students to continue with their non-attention. Your presence is reinforced by being the person in the room demanding attention, asking questions and fielding replies. Additionally, you may be the person who refocuses attention, summarizes and points to things. All these activities signal to the students who is in charge. If you are active rather than passive, assertive rather than a shrinking violet, you can look and sound like a teacher who has real presence. There is no need to enter the class-room carrying a lighted firework in each hand, but you certainly need to look as if you mean business. You will need more than a smile, and may need to hassle dawdlers, returning to a positive businesslike presence.

Learn to persist until you have students' attention

The most common two problems for a beginner are signalling effectively that you want attention, then making sure that they have eye-contact with your students before continuing. You take centre stage, but your students' attention is elsewhere. You will find that you cannot take centre stage and simply wait. In many instances you cannot signal that you want attention and wait forever. Students will need to be diverted from whatever else they are doing. Some trainees complain that it is impossible to get students to turn towards a whiteboard or to give their full attention. If you believe that students pay attention with their backs towards you, then you will never get them to pay attention. Insist on full attention from the very first moment that you stand in front of a class, persisting for however long it takes. Why would you want that? When you explain or ask questions, your facial expression is very important, as is your tone of voice. If there is no eye-contact, then having a good rapport with your students is almost impossible. Facial expression, a raised eyebrow or a smile communicate with your students. No student is going to engage with these unless they are actually looking at you. You may not always achieve 100 percent eye-contact, but there are known bad habits that students will display if you ask them to listen without looking.

At worst, eye-contact from students might be a glazed look of inattention, but more likely it indicates some level of involvement. It is not a foolproof signal they are paying attention but it is more convincing than the backs of their heads. At worst, students sit with their backs to the teacher, chatter while the teacher is speaking and fidget with equipment in their hands. Sometimes their idea of paying attention is a reluctant half-turn towards the teacher or board. The general 'under-chatter' then becomes accepted with the teacher's voice loud enough to drown it out. Students fiddle with pencils, paper, or even with another's hairstyle instead of listening, and anything else you care to imagine. Another might wander over to another part of the room for no good reason. Two more might play a subversive touch game of 'You're it' and another might construct an abstract piece of origami with scrap paper. Contrast this with students who, in the first few seconds of your teaching, have realized that you meant business and were not prepared to let them continue with their private agenda of non-attention.

Many trainee teachers are quite unused to a public style of speaking to a large group and are surprised to hear the words come out of their mouth. If the signal you give for getting attention is your own voice, then have a con-sistent, strong way of stopping the class or group. Imagine a typical situation where there is some general class chatter going on, too loud for the teacher to be heard using a normal speaking voice. One teacher's method of signalling is to shout 'Thank you', another might be 'Everybody stop. Things down, and look this way.' Another claps their hands three times and says 'Looking and listening please.' Another taps on a chime bar, another a small bell, and yet another slams a piece of wood on a desk (a little overdramatic but still effective). Give a clear, loud signal, wait and drop the volume of your voice. Make sure if you clap your hands that you speak loudly at the same time otherwise the students may well clap back, mimicking your signal.

You may not need to rush out to buy a gavel, but whatever strong signal you try, you may be sure of one thing. It is not the signal that matters so much as what the students have learned that it *means*. If your signal means nothing to them you can stamp and scream all you like to no effect. If you want to use your voice, your speech signal must be the same each time, generally loud, followed by a pause, followed by a drop in the volume of your voice. You may even need to rehearse what this means with students, for example:

> When I say ... it *means* that you turn round, face me and put everything out of your hands. Push things on your desk away from you so you don't fiddle with them. All eyes this way and ready to concentrate.

Knowing what the signal actually means will work for most children if you are consistent. The time to do all this is the very *first* time you ask a class to pay attention. No need to sound tetchy, but every need to sound businesslike.

> I think what I've learned most is to persist. If you do that for long enough, they [students] eventually give in. I might give them grief about losing time, but day-by-day they know I mean what I say. I do sound determined to get attention as well as persisting, and I move on quickly as soon as I have them looking and listening. (Newly-qualified teacher)

Young children are likely to respond to a different approach, but the signal is still a strong one:

> I wave a magic wand and this means I want my five wishes. These are: (1) eyes look-ing at me; (2) ears listening; (3) lips closed; (4) sitting up straight; (5) hands in laps. The children probably think, 'The old bat's waving her wand again', but it does seem to work if you follow it up with praise for those who respond quickly. (Infant school headteacher)

> I found that, specifically when on the carpet, instead of just getting the children's atten-tion by nagging or keep saying 'Eyes this way . . !' if you carry out a series of actions such as 'Hands on your head, on your knees, touch your nose (these can be more sophisti-cated depending on the age. For example, 'Put your left hand on your right knee' and so on. Finish with fingers over your lips, lowering the tone and volume of your voice) and 'Hands in your laps . . .', I have found this really works, especially at times when children need to sit for long periods of time. (Trainee teacher)

What these last two approaches have in common is that they engage the child's mind, preventing it from wandering. In the physical 'Simon Says' approach, there are quick-thinking actions needed so students become very involved. They are engaged in a lively game so it is difficult not to pay attention. The magic wand works because of what it means. The 'Simon Says' game has other varia-tions, one of which is to get students to put their hand on their T-shirt logo to show they are ready. Next time maybe it will be: 'Put your hand on your right shoulder.' The most mechanistic strategy I ever saw came from a teacher who said: 'Eyes on the ceiling. Eyes on the floor. Eyes on me.' It still worked.

The power of a pause

Technically, the crucial feature of getting attention is to pause after the strong attention signal, and insist until you have eye-contact and all chatter, 'pen-maintenance' and fidgeting has stopped. It is tempting to settle for less (seriously disturbed students notwithstanding) but in time you will undermine your signal if you give way. Insist, insist and insist by saying the same phrase, such as 'I can't see everyone's eyes.' Pause, repeat the phrase with slight surprise in your voice, and insist. You may not succeed in this every time, but you are developing and honing a basic classroom skill. There is also a curious effect (which I have yet to disprove): if your signal is to clap your hands or bang an object three times, the pace of this has to be right. Three overly rapid sounds really count as one. You need to clap your hands at a pace of one loud sound per second, not four sounds or two sounds and always followed by a one or two-second pause before instructions. I must have explained this signal to trainee teachers hundreds of times, but they still misunderstand. They start their lesson when students are not ready and allow chatter and inattention. Double the amount of time you intend to persist with your strong signal and that will be about right.

A common error some beginners make, when they signal and wait, is to be sucked into responding to questions (diversions again). Resist taking any notice of 'Please Miss, I haven't got a . . .' questions and keep strictly focused. If you want to add a gesture, make a non-verbal 'stop' signal with your hand in front of the child's face. Your 'stop' signal means 'not now'. Logically the last thing you want to do is encourage students to gain your attention when actually you are trying to gain theirs. You need full attention, nothing else. If you put up with under-chatter while you speak loudly, students are going to think that you are willing to compete with them. They will think that you do not mind talking while they talk, or that you are willing to speak even louder so that they can still chatter. Exclude all extra noise, close the door and sometimes even a window to make sure there are no distractions. You can then sense the atmosphere and make listening a priority.

The mid-sentence pause

- Stop mid-sentence and call the student's name.
- Pause and repeat *only the name* until you have attention (ignore a response such as an impolite 'What?' or 'What!' or 'Not doing nuffin').
- Slow down your speech and (possibly) add a hint of gravitas. Be ready for an interruption such as 'Wasn't me!' and override it with, for example, 'Maybe it wasn't, but what are you doing that we don't like?'
- Spell out exactly what you want, emphasizing work, listening, concentrating, thinking. Make this a maximum of 20 seconds, ending with a reminder about the task or need for attention.

Some teachers actually pause for extra effect once they have got attention. They also stretch a mid-sentence pause as long as they can. This is only acting, but it has a strong controlling effect on a class. A teacher who pauses for effect is not the same as one who pauses and slows the pace of the lesson. Be very careful to keep up a lively pace after pausing or you will lose your momentum.

A pause for effect is a contrast with the pace that goes before and after it. Pausing effectively has the bonus that it can make you appear confidently in charge. When you have gained attention there is a vacuum waiting to be filled. Fill it, and move on or your class will switch to their own agenda.

Persisting is not always waiting

> Persist and insist. I know I should do this, but in my case it's become a pace-killing wait. Starting the class by grabbing their attention and creating some excitement before tackling chatting and fidgeting is something I'm going to try. (Trainee teacher)

> You see trainees waiting forever and saying things like 'Who remembers our rule about listening?' Then they go through the listening rule again, by which time the mutterings have begun and the attention they want is half-hearted. Why do they do that? You don't see experienced teachers do it, and they are still able to get attention. That's because they move swiftly on when most children are looking, and after a few seconds speak sharply to anyone who still isn't paying attention. The clever ones check again after a few seconds and round up the strays. (Education lecturer)

You probably want to widen the range of your attention-getting skills and will need to think of alternatives to waiting for attention. The key thing is: move it on! You can get serious and wait for attention, but there is also something to be said for taking students by surprise and getting them involved in spite of themselves. The more you leave gaps, the more chance there is to have to discipline students instead of getting down to some teaching.

Gaining attention without waiting forever

Some teachers sweep into the classroom already greeting their students as they move to take centre stage. They look as if they are about to enjoy what they are going to do. They signal for attention and continue loudly while writing on the board. They direct attention by pointing and saying 'Everyone looking at this list of words here' and only then do they turn to look at the class. Waiting for attention has been deferred. Part-way through their explanation, they persist in getting full attention by pausing, scanning the room and rounding up strays by saying something like 'John, Peter, Anna. We've *already* started and I need your attention now.' The pace is brisk. They pause again and ask a question, pause mid-sentence and scan the whole class again for eye-contact. But they still persist until they have attention, gradually raising the concentration level, smiling and continuing. The volume of their voice drops and the session becomes interactive with students being chosen to respond to directions, questions or problems to solve. These teachers engage students before they quite know what has hit them, then stop to round up the strays.

A beginner in the classroom is more likely to signal and wait, but you can try other ways so long as you still persist within the first few minutes. An experienced teacher has already-established routines and expectations. Persisting is not something you do only at the beginning of a lesson. You will need to persist at any point in the lesson should you need students to listen and respond. Stop the lesson dead in its tracks when you want to regain attention.

Persistence and power struggles

Some students want to be the last to give their attention, an irritating event for you as the teacher. Their behaviour can be refusal to give eye-contact, sometimes under-chatter, sometimes a power struggle over equipment. This may be about being the last to close a storage drawer or the very last to put down pens or pencils. Some students (very few in fact) may need to be ignored if they are known to be extreme in their behaviour. Whatever the ploy, very early intervention for the majority of students is more effective than endless patience and a frustrated 'I'm waiting' expression on your face. This might take the form of a sharp reprimand, backed up by a threat of losing five minutes at break or playtime. More likely a threat of losing some opportunity to do something very enjoyable that the rest of the class is going to do will have the desired effect. Give a warning, however, and a choice such as 'You're choosing to lose some of your time if you . . .'. The advantage of appearing to turn this into a choice (which it is not) is that you shift responsibility for the consequences to the child.

Your persistence with dawdlers and power-strugglers needs to have consequences without the class atmosphere becoming negative. It is better to build an early expectation that around 30 seconds is long enough before dawdlers hear you say 'Quickly you two, let's not have you choosing to make up time later on.' You will need to back this up with a name on the board or a warning about making up time that you are prepared to carry out. It is not so much your tone of voice that has an effect, more the realization that you really will carry out any threats. The longer you let inattention go on without an immediate warning, the more likely the problem is to escalate. If students know that there will be consequences they dislike, they will opt for an easier way out. Some teachers have a plan for students to earn time back by the break: 'You might earn breaktime back if you're sensible for the rest of the lesson.' Alongside this you can remind consistently about 'being cooperative', 'concentrating' and spell out as positively as you can the classroom social skills you want to develop.

Strategies to avoid anger

A teacher's anger rewards bad behaviour, so it should be displayed rarely. Students mirror anger inside even if they seem cowed by it on the outside. The price you pay for angry confrontation if you win is resentment from the student on the receiving end. If you are angry inside and do not want to show it, look for something elsewhere to praise, shifting the focus of your mind from behaviour that you dislike to behaviour that you can praise. Resist the temptation to play what you think is the role of a very strict and slightly aggressive teacher, or you will shout 'Ross! That's *one* minute off your breaktime!' If you overreact, you will sound out of control yourself rather than in control of the lesson. It is far better to opt for a determined 30-second speech that emphasizes the third person as the acceptable goodie. It is better to say 'In this class *we* don't behave like that because . . .', 'I need you to . . .' and 'When we're all ready . . .' instead of personally-directed insults. You will achieve nothing by saying 'You little aphid!' or 'Stop behaving like an animal and I won't have to treat you like one, will I?' A difficult child is more likely to mimic an animal in response to being called one. Criticize the action, not the actor. Use the third person 'We', rather than 'You' and spell out clearly the consistent option of 'Work now, or lose time later.'

Anger escalates a difficult situation into an impossible one. If anyone is going to interrupt an angry student, it has to be you. Interrupt with 'I'm talking, you're listening', retaining your gravitas and slow, calm delivery. Despite the stress level involved, keep calm and maintain a positive atmosphere. Your success here is not judged on whether your strategy worked brilliantly but whether you remained outwardly calm (I have used this strategy and usually it has succeeded). If you know the student well and have a good relationship, you could finish by injecting humour to lighten the situation. You could say, for example, 'Fairynuffski, we're done talking about this. Let's get back to work.' Remain positive and you will win through. Become angry and you will lose.

A further strategy for avoiding anger is to tell yourself: 'It's only behaviour and I need to deal with it.' When you first begin teaching, there are dozens of situations that you will find uncomfortable because you are seeing them for the first time as a teacher. A couple of years into the profession you will think differently because you have adjusted to the reality of seeing similar situations develop in your classroom. You will be better at allowing cooling-off time for students and softening your voice.

A stress-busting strategy

Stress often arises from the way that you respond to events. Changing the habits of a student or a class means that you will need to change how you respond to what usually happens.

> I've got this stress-buster from the headteacher. Whenever you've got a behaviour problem, such as Adam, who gets out of his seat and will not sit down, or he's cheeky, it is seriously stressful. So later on, you write down 'When Adam gets out of his seat and it winds me up, instead of saying . . . I will . . .' then you write down another response, such

as 'When Adam gets cheeky, I'll say, "We'll discuss your out-of-seat behaviour and bad manners at the end of the lesson." And if that doesn't work, you write another response, such as 'When Adam is cheeky, I'll say, "You'll miss the best activities and have to sit writing by yourself if your manners don't improve." You keep going. But you must put it down on paper. It really works! (Trainee teacher)

The strategy that works is to write:

- Whenever (the student's behaviour) . . .
- Instead of (my current behaviour) . . .
- I will (a different response) . . .

What you are doing through this strategy is changing your behaviour when the student least expects it. You are already prepared for the next 'wind-up'. At the very least, you are preventing yourself from stress by having something else to say or do. The act of writing it down confirms in your mind what you will do. Also, it may serve as a rapid reminder at the start of your lesson. The student's behaviour acts as a trigger to the prepared self-script instead of a trigger to stress.

Respond quickly to changing events

An experienced teacher seems to be able to spot trouble before it starts and avoid it escalating. Experience will lead you to listen for different sounds being made and scan for evidence of off-task behaviour. You can scan the room, dislike what you see and decide how to take action. This may mean that you speak to a student without giving any eye-contact whatsoever. Your intervention is minimal because you appear to be far more absorbed with other things and too busy to deal with minor infringements of behaviour code. You say what you need to happen with the full expectation that it is going to be done.

Eyes in the back of your head

Ruby is off-task and no longer concentrating. You notice this as you scan the room and do not like what you see.

- Turn your back on Ruby and move away.
- Without looking, sharply speak to Ruby and say 'Ruby, I need you to concentrate.'
- Keep your back towards Ruby and wait about 30 seconds.
- Check to see if Ruby is back on task.
- Go over to Ruby and give her some positive feedback when you can.

Reacting quickly to changing events means that you are in tune with what is going on around you, especially responses to the activities that you have set up. There is no need to go looking for trouble, but every need to recognize when students have had enough and need a change of emphasis in their lesson. There is every need to praise good efforts as you scan your classroom. Teachers who react quickly to events actually *prevent* trouble because they move on and involve their students in something else. This is not a matter of darting your head in all directions. Effective scanning is a thorough, more searching browse of the class at frequent intervals to stay in tune with what is going on and pick up what is not. You scan to pick up on the body language, fidgets and excited learners. The remainder is done by listening to comments, noises and chair-shuffling, all of which are signals. Reacting quickly is about anticipating what is needed next in the lesson. Sometimes it is about reacting to demands by saying 'I can't get to you all at once, so don't keep calling out my name.'

> I usually know who to watch carefully to prevent trouble. Once you get to know the kids you can actually anticipate problems. Most of the difficult kids are *really* bad at hiding the signals they give off. So you can tell by what they do with equipment or how they sit what mood they're in. Most of my little criminals are rumbled before they even know it. (Year 6 teacher)

Reacting quickly is rather like taking the class pulse. Second-by-second you sense the atmosphere and check that the heart rate has not reached danger point. Most difficult students need a very early signal that you are on their case. A misconception you might have is that reacting quickly means you do things more quickly. You can react quickly and actually appear to take no action at all. Reacting quickly is rapidly registering what is happening around you and taking a decision about what to do next. That decision might be to take immediate strong action, change the direction of the lesson, or signal that there is very little time left to complete work.

> Sometimes I'll say 'I hope you won't need a warning because I don't really want that to happen.' In fact I've just given a warning of sorts, but not yet gone down an all-too-familiar route to punishment! (Newly-qualified teacher)

Reducing stress by planning for variety

There is hardly anything worse for a child than to fail at something that the teacher has described as 'fun' and 'easy'. Certainly, you would learn this the hard way if you tried to please students all the time. Variety has nothing to do with being a stage performer in the classroom. Students are there to learn and you cannot deliver from the expectation that everything is interesting and good fun all day. A great deal of what happens in school is hard because it is hard and for no other reason. You can please some of the students for some of the time. Variety is more about judging when to change direction, when to begin a new task and how many different activities will go on in your lesson.

Good lesson planning is the main component of good behaviour management. A well-planned and motivating lesson can remove the need to manage behaviour and therefore help you to keep your cool. You do not need to plan for students as if they have no attention-span, but you do need to see your lesson from their point of view. If you transmit the idea that nothing students do should ever take more than five minutes, it is likely that they will behave as if this is true. You can always set students a task and build in a few interludes, stopping them, asking questions and returning to the same task with fresh enthusiasm.

> I think if a beginner keeps young children on the carpeted area for 45 minutes they are really asking for trouble. However enthusiastic you sound, it's just too long. Twenty minutes will do, and you need to finish by setting tasks and making sure the children understand. They need to know where equipment is and what to do with it. Young children are doers more than listeners, so usually they can't wait to get their hands on something. (Infant teacher)

Think of yourself timing the learning rather than timing the lesson. If your introduction is too short, students will not know what to do and if it is too long, they will forget what has been said. Professional judgement is all about making good decisions about how to balance talking, listening and doing. There are no hard-and-fast rules about this, but long introductions stretch attention-span to the limit. As will be explained in other chapters, there are alternatives to the long introduction. What would happen, for example, if you planned your introduction then halved it? You could come back to the second half later in the lesson, or split your introduction into three phases. One of the most effective science lessons I ever observed was one where students began with an activity that they did not understand. They had to connect a battery, switch and bulb without instructions, then were called to the carpeted area for the introduction to a project about electrical circuits. The teacher had written on the whiteboard: 'Find out how to connect the switch, battery, wires and bulb.' There is always more than one way to do things.

Questions for reflection

- How might you practise a strong signal for getting attention?
- What signals do other teachers use?
- How important is it to plan for variety as well as content?
- What is effective scanning of a class?
- What are the alternatives to waiting patiently for attention?
- What behaviour are you ignoring and therefore tolerating?
- How can you appear more confident when you take centre stage?
- How can you sustain a presence in the classroom when students are working at a task?

Checklist summary

- Avoid the classic irrational belief that students *should never* be bored and your lesson *should* be brilliant.
- The first stage in getting attention is to give a very clear signal that students can hear, or a well-established visual signal.
- Teachers who react quickly to events actually prevent trouble because they move on and involve their students.
- When you have gained attention there is a vacuum waiting to be filled. Fill it, and move on or your class will switch to their own agenda.
- Effective scanning is a thorough, more searching browse of the class at frequent intervals to stay in tune with what is going on, and pick up what is not.
- Reacting quickly is rapidly registering what is happening around you and taking a decision about what to do next.
- Never underestimate the power of a pause, but be very careful to keep up a lively pace after pausing, or you will lose your momentum.
- If you ignore misbehaviour that is likely to escalate, you only signal that you tolerate it.
- Think of yourself timing the learning, rather than timing the lesson.
- Learn to persist until you have students' attention.
- Plan for learning, not just to interest and please students.
- Give plenty of feedback about work and effort.

3 Routines, scripts and 'teacher-talk'

Routines from the outset

Your job is to establish routines, through taking advice from more experienced colleagues if you are a trainee. Everything you say and do sets patterns which can become ingrained, so developing good 'teacher-talk' is important for success. Every teacher has a few well-tried scripts and phrases that they trot out in different situations. This teacher-talk is a specific way of phrasing instructions and directions. Phrases beginning 'I need you to . . .', 'You can *when* . . .' or 'When I tell you . . .' are typical of teacher-talk. These, and a certain 'teacher' tone of voice, become so deeply ingrained that some experienced teachers find it difficult to switch off. Their teaching voice can be overheard in more public places such as the school staffroom, a department store or supermarket checkout. Their voice is loud and its volume does not change despite circumstances. As a trainee recently remarked: 'I must be changing into a teacher, because my boyfriend can't understand why I'm saying things to him like "I need you to" and sounding so bossy.'

By the time you arrive in school as a trainee teacher you will see a class that is already beginning to be established in their routines. There is 'carpet behaviour', 'on-task behaviour' and routines for things such as leaving a room. Experienced teachers like at least a couple of weeks to get their class to respond in the way they want. You will rarely see how this has been achieved because you are not there from the outset. Many newly-qualified teachers, in their first full-time post, have been misled into thinking that they have an ideal class and can relax their vigilance. If you are newly qualified, expect to be tried out, but see this as your opportunity to build habits without making too much of a fuss about them. If you have thought carefully about what you want to happen, you will know already what the class routines are likely to be. Your job as a teacher is to establish habits, demonstrate them and stick to them over a period of weeks.

Setting patterns

A new teacher, Brad, faces his class for the first time, smiles and immediately begins asking questions, only accepting answers from students who have a hand up. Later he finds out a few names and tells the class who he is. He praises the class for having the courage to answer questions so well when they do not know him.

Another new teacher, Andy, faces his class for the first time, gains attention and silence. He tells the class his name, smiles and explains a few rules about what he expects. He clamps down on any chatter and begins to explain how climate change is affecting the world. He asks questions and checks understanding.

Yet another new teacher, Katrina, has decided to meet her new class by beginning with a short practical activity. She provides some quiz sheets about the weather and mixed-up answers printed on slips of paper. She stresses cooperation and taking turns. She tells the class that they have to work things out for themselves. Later, she tells the class about herself and finds out a few student names.

Each of these new teachers is setting a pattern by the emphasis they give to their initial teaching. None of these is actually better than any other and there will be many other ways used by an individual teacher. Patterns begin to be set when it becomes clear how one teacher prefers a regimented approach, while another wants an immediately interactive dialogue with their class. Whatever you decide to do in the first few days with a new class sets patterns for future lessons.

Once routines become more of a habit, you have probably handed over responsibility to students for sticking to them. However, routines fail if you have not sorted out clearly in your own mind what you want to achieve. If you have a personal rule that nobody runs into or out of a room and you allow a student to do that, you transmit a message that it does not matter. Remember: if you stand firm when you establish a routine, it will happen. If you give way, you blur the routine and it will fail.

Beginners most often fail because they are not firm enough about blocking students' attempts to 'torpedo' routines. Calling out is a good example. Beginners start with good intentions, but then allow a few individuals to call out. This may seem innocent enough because the question-and-answer routine is going well, but it sends out the wrong message. The few individuals who call out will become the majority and the routine will never be successfully established. Beginners also fail to see when they are being diverted (see Chapter 2). Children often arrive with an agenda of things to tell the teacher and things to ask. They pick their moment, usually one when you are trying to get their attention. Sometimes students trot out their agenda before you even have the chance to gain attention to make a start. When the city football team wins a match, maybe you will need to know that, but not right now.

If you want to waste your breath, say 'Don't call out', or worse still, 'How many times have I told you . . .?' This does not direct students' behaviour in any purposeful way. Better teacher-talk is, for example, 'Hands up, who can tell me . . .?', which is different from 'Tell me who . . .'. Hearing the word 'tell' may invite calling out (telling) unless the student has the wit to remember to put up a hand. 'Hands only' or a signal such as your hand raised to exemplify this can reinforce the routine. Yes, it is very boring to sustain this, but if you waver then you no longer have a meaningful reference point. If you say 'We put our hands up' you do not want to find that privately one or two students are saying 'She doesn't really mean that.' When you say 'We put our hands up', it is only a reminder. The class will understand how important this is to you if you persist and demonstrate the routine by not accepting answers from students who call out.

Dealing with calling out is actually a good opportunity to send out a clear signal when you are new to a class. There will be plenty of students who forget to put up a hand and call out instead (trainee teachers are notoriously poor at allowing this to continue). From the outset, you need to put your hand in front of any student who calls out, blocking the answer. Do this like a *stop* signal and turn towards anyone else who has their hand up. When you block students who call out, you send a strong signal. You may think you need to tell them why they are being blocked, but believe me, they usually know. Occasionally, there is a child who simply wants you to see that she is bright enough to answer and takes little notice of the hands-up rule. You may need a minor behaviour plan such as: 'Lucy, next time you feel like calling out, say to yourself, "*Stop* or my teacher won't ask me any more." Alternatively, you may need to establish a private reminder for Lucy, a particular signal such as a handclap, clicker, hand turned in a particular direction or an easily-marked tally chart. This will almost certainly need reinforcing with rewards and sanctions (see Chapter 6).

A summary of 'hands up'

Practise refusing eye-contact, not even looking in the direction of the culprit who calls out. Meanwhile, give positive reinforcement of 'hands up' to reward those who do so, as in 'That's right, David, and thanks for putting your hand up'. As soon as a student who previously called out puts up their hand, respond positively by thanking them too. This is important because you do not want them to think 'Well, I put my hand up but I still got ignored'.

- Ignore calling out by refusing eye-contact.
- Block with a hand signal (palm facing them as a *stop* signal)
- Give low-level thanks to students who put up their hands.
- Watch for the first hand to go up from the hardcore of callers.
- Thank them too.

In one primary school I visited, the routine first thing in the morning was that students walked quietly into the room, got out their class reading book and started to read it. Another school had a system of five minutes settling time followed by the register, during which students were silent and looked at their personal list of spellings to learn them. Infant school children started their day by drawing, doing a puzzle or assembling Lego bricks. When the register was called, they were on the carpeted area with mouths closed and hands in their laps ready to listen. Some schools have students line up in the playground before coming into the school. Other schools are less formal but still have clearly understood habits about who sits where and how students come into a room.

> I have three difficult boys in my Year 1 class so I've created three magic spots on the carpet area to separate them. They know they have to sit on the magic spot and I tell them it's 'because it makes you behave like magic!' Crazy things work, don't they? (Year 1 teacher)

Sometimes routines are accompanied by a well-honed script. This can be a shorthand phrase such as 'Litter off the floor, ready to go.' If you want cooperation with your routines, a great deal depends on the relationship that you develop with your students. One thing you can do is to get involved with clubs, football, netball or anything that helps you to be seen in a more positive light (see Chapter 1). That way you are not just someone who might be seen as bossy and slightly formal. If you cannot do that you will need to rely on being positive and demonstrate that you are human, not a cardboard cutout. Anything you can do to break down barriers and work alongside students is going to help develop a good relationship. Helping with a school play or musical event, discussing interests such as students' domestic pets and showing interest in their lives creates a better working relationship.

'When . . . then' as a scripted pattern

A useful phrase for establishing working patterns as a new teacher is to begin your instructions with 'When you are working with me . . .'. This clears the decks for you to establish your own reasonable routines and expectations. As a child, you might remember parents and teachers using a 'When . . . then' pattern, as in: 'When you've finished your food then you can switch on the television', or 'When you've calmed down, I'll think about speaking to you.' This device is used to combat unreasonable requests to shoot off immediately and do something, meanwhile leaving equipment and litter around the room. It may also be useful for sharing equipment, as in: 'Simon, you can use the stapler *when* Darren's finished with it.'

The scripted phrase can sound very positive, as in: 'Yes, you certainly can when you've finished chewing.' What students hear is 'you can', instead of a blank 'not until you'. Older students are rather more wise to this device, but it still has its place if you can play a few variations such as 'Yes, Ben. I'd really like you to do that when you've finished sorting out your maths corrections.' Usually you can increase the power of the praise that you give at the start of a comment that you know is not quite what the student wanted to hear, as in: 'I can see how well you're doing with your work and I'm really impressed with your concentration. As soon as you've finished it, you can certainly help in the library.'

Every trainee teacher makes mistakes in the way that they script their instructions. Children tend to hear the first three words and act on them. There is no guarantee, but try saying 'You can all go when I'm ready' without there being a rustle of movement before you reach the word 'when'. Your hope may be that students possess good social skills and are self-disciplined, but many are not remotely like that. For example, you are teaching a class of seven-year-olds and it is approaching lunchtime. You might have decided to let the best behaved table or row leave first. How you do this is up to you, but certainly there is a difference between saying 'Off you go', and 'That table can put chairs underneath.' If you say 'Off you go', most likely students will make a rush for the door unless you already have established a polite way of room-quitting. If all you say is 'Put your chairs under the desks', there's nothing much they can do but stand and wait for the next instruction, which is 'Quietly walk out.' Unfortunately, a great deal of class management is a matter of using the exact words for the effect that you want. Often, experienced teachers are heard saying '*Quietly* walk out', rather than 'Walk out quietly', so that their students (in theory) register the operative word before they hear the remainder. As an exercise you might try completing the following, and making them part of your daily personal scripting.

- When you're looking this way . . .
- When I can see all eyes . . .
- When I can hear the silence . . .
- When there are no feet fidgeting . . .
- When you go to your desks . . .
- When you've finished that . . .
- You can when . . .
- We will when . . .
- Just before we do that, we need to . . .

Spelling out what you want

The following script is a typical example of a teacher's call for attention and class monitoring – it has been included here because some beginners take time to develop appropriate teacher-talk. Besides this, your very first moments in front of a new class may not be your most confident ones.

A script is not a complete cure for the nerves, but it can help you to understand what you are aiming for. As with any script, much depends on how you use it, particularly your pace and the voice tone. No script is going to fit every occasion because you are working with children, not robots. For example, you would need a slightly different approach with a reception class, or Year 1, so the script provided here is not set in stone. You may think, 'When do I pause?', 'When do I crank up the pace and move the script on?' The answer lies within yourself and you will need to adapt, experiment, sense the atmosphere and change what you say. Inevitably, you will need to change your voice tone and manner according to the age-group that you are teaching.

The main strategy used in this example is one of persisting until students believe that you mean what you say. This involves the use of words and phrases that spell out what you want. The script begins with a strong signal, which might be your voice or something else to make a distinctive sound (see Chapter 2). You might draw a clock on the board or count down loudly to zero. All these signals are possible but choose one that will not have you counting zero when the class is still very noisy. Imagine you have just taken centre stage. You have positioned yourself so that you have good eye-contact and can see all the students in the class. Watch for the 'positive pause' later in the script.

Script for Year 5

(Refers to several possible curriculum subjects as examples)

> Teacher: Looking and listening please. Pens and pencils down, sitting up straight, eyes this way.
>
> *[Pause, during which there is shuffling and under-chatter.]*
>
> Teacher: Haven't got all eyes. Brilliant! I can see Mary, Jon, Rachel are ready. I need you listening, concentrating and looking at me. *[lower volume of voice. A boy makes noises]*
>
> Teacher: *[voice quieter if possible, but with plenty of businesslike pace]* You're choosing to lose time. Quickly. Concentrating, sitting properly and ready now, mouths closed and eyes this way looking at me. Hands and feet to yourself.
>
> Child: But Miss, we don't . . .
>
> Child: I haven't got a . . .
>
> Child: Can we . . .
>
> Teacher: *[uses hand to convey 'stop' signal, lowers voice to serious low level]* Questions later. I expect politeness and concentration. I've had to speak to you already and I expect you to be ready.
>
> *[Pause, pause, scan the class and wait/or impose sanction if necessary. Persist.]*
>
> Teacher: Excuse me Simon, you're still not concentrating. *[Possible sanction warning, e.g. name on the board as a warning]*
>
> *[As soon as there is silence, give a 'positive pause' by smiling, relaxing the atmosphere and saying:]*

Teacher: Good. We're ready. Hands up who can tell me . . . still listening please, Simon . . . how might we begin to do the subtraction from the larger numbers on the whiteboard. Hands only.

It might be, for younger children, 'Fold your arms, look at me and listen . . . do you remember yesterday we found . . .', 'I have something amazing to show you . . . ', 'I want you to imagine . . .' or 'I am going to ask you to do something and you only have one minute to do it', but body language, eye contact, facial expressions and humour all help, as does pre-empting behaviour, e.g. 'You don't need to ask Jane anything at the moment [*child just about to lean across*], you need to listen to me.'

[*If a student thinks they can call across the room to another or make a stupid noise, be on to this like lightning.*]

Teacher: [*very quickly this time*] Max, don't delay us. We use quieter voices and not across the room. That is unacceptable and holding us up. Now tell me yourself [*target the student*] how many bones in a giraffe's neck? [*there are exactly the same number of bones as in a human being, seven in all*]

[*Assume attention is flagging*]

Teacher: Concentrating, thinking hard. You might know the answer to this . . . hands up who can . . . Sophie, sitting properly please . . . everybody thinking, concentrating and tell me why the temperature of the water changes so quickly . . .

And so on . . .

Avoid the chatline, no extra words – just repeat what you want. In time students might repeat back your favourite phrases such as 'That's not acceptable', or 'Unacceptable behaviour!' but you need to ignore this or quietly say 'Yes, that's right. You're beginning to understand.' If you want to remain consistent, never negotiate about behaviour. There will be far more appropriate times to negotiate learning instead. Give students time to respond to your request of course, but hold fast to your intentions. Students benefit hugely from consistent and habit-forming routines. They particularly need to know the difference between interactive involvement, where they speak a great deal, and needing to listen attentively.

The pen-fiddlers mentioned in the previous chapter can be hard to crack. Some students are hardly capable of listening without touching equipment so there are two additional ruses you might like to try. The first is to have a signal that means 'push equipment away from you so you do not touch it' and the short-cut for an individual student can be 'Jessica. Resist!' The second is to have a doodle-pad for each student and a system where they can doodle as they listen, but not take their pen to pieces. This is more difficult to manage and has the disadvantage that students do not give eye-contact when you most need it. Other than these, you are rather stuck with a career in which you will constantly monitor pen-fiddling students, pausing mid-sentence to say things such as 'I can see too many pen-fiddlers'. All this may seem trivial, but if you clamp down on fidgets and pen-fiddlers, you send out a message that you want things done well.

What will you forget? You will gain attention, direct eyes to the whiteboard but *fail to check* that children are actually doing this. I have seen beginners steamroller their way through a lesson without pausing to check their students are still with them. The reason why you keep checking to make sure that students are with you is that you will never sustain their attention unless you do. Assume that they have a private agenda just waiting to take over when they get the chance. They will chatter, daydream, think about relationships, food and anything that takes the focus of their attention elsewhere. We all do this at some time or other. Check and keep checking.

> When I first visited my teaching practice school, I walked past the assembly hall where 'Mrs Miller' had Year 3 there sitting on the floor with their backs like ramrods. 'How does she do that?', I asked my teacher, who replied, 'Well. That's how she wants them to sit, so they do, don't they.' (Trainee teacher)

Giving empty threats

The script for Year 5 includes an inevitable amount of waiting time. An alternative to this has already been mentioned in Chapter 2 where the teacher swept into the room and the lesson was quickly under way. The bus always needs to keep moving along. Students soon sense how long you are prepared to wait before you impose a first warning or threaten a sanction. You can try to involve them despite themselves and quickly move to the work, but you still may need to impose warnings sooner rather than later. A very early warning of sanctions is far more effective than a late one. Late warnings are followed almost inevitably by a sanction to prove that you mean what you say. In most situations of disruption I have observed I would have threatened with a warning much earlier than trainees do. Warnings are better than surprise sanctions, such as an immediate five minutes off breaktime. If you impose a sanction before a warning, this causes resentment.

Freya's tally chart

You may constantly revisit the 'That's a minute off your breaktime' in an attempt to reduce the time you wait for the class to stop yapping and listen. You end up missing your break too, and it punishes many children who have not been talking. Freya, a Year 4 teacher, has a great system for a noisy class – an interruptions chart. It is simply a table with a column for names and a tally column. Each tally equals two minutes off lunchtime, and five tallies is an automatic detention. Afternoon tallies carry over to the next day. The advantages of this system are that:

- lunchtime is a much greater loss than break, because of games club and lunch;
- it targets the real culprits (the students who have to be commenting and gossiping *all the time*) and not the body of the class;
- it's novel, and that always helps, and few students want to go beyond two tallies.

If a student knows that you will review your decision about a sanction at the end of a lesson it can have a positive effect on that student's work. Whenever you warn and threaten sanctions inevitably you are creating a less rewarding atmosphere. Sanctions are necessary and difficult students invite negative responses. This leaves you with a deficit that needs to be repaired quickly by finding opportunities to praise. Freya's tally chart (see above) gives her students a generous five chances and a clear signal that consequences will be carried out. Its success depends on students losing time that they really do not want to, especially time away from friends in the middle of the day. Freya can tally and praise almost in the same breath. Her threats are always carried out.

Keeping on top of a good start

Sustaining attention requires more subtle scripting. You will need to engage children's minds in several ways because managing a class cannot be separated from ongoing work. Think of the three main points that you want to get across to students in your lesson. If you do this, you are bound to emphasize something as being more important. Some beginners create problems for themselves by blurring their objectives. If you know what your main focus is, this will creep into your teacher-talk and give your lesson some shape. Here is where three additional techniques come to the fore. The first is to refocus attention as it wanes. Typically, you will begin to explain, question or instruct and three or more students will look away or chatter. Within a nanosecond of this happening, refocus attention in as unobtrusive a way as you can. You do not want to stop and remonstrate or you will lose the thread of your lesson. A sharp 'Simon. Looking this way' will work if it is done soon enough. Avoid constant interruptions to the flow, but keep refocusing attention periodically as you go. The second is to engage students' thinking. When teachers engage minds, typically they use classroom language in their script such as:

Imagine . . .
I want you to think about . . .
If I had 12 pieces of pizza and . . .
I wonder who knows if . . .
Here's a problem we need to solve . . .
And the third planet from the Sun is . . . ?
If you were on the bottom of the sea and . . .
If the hands on this clock said . . .

The third is to use directive language, which is language to focus students' eyes and attention specifically. Directive language makes teacher-talk specific by asking precisely for the desired behaviour and action. Here are some examples which specifically direct mind, eyes and ears. (Most experienced teachers, by the way, would probably do this without realizing that they did it.)

Look at the speech bubble halfway down the page ... (rather than 'Look at the page').
Look at the top left line on the board where it says ... (rather than 'Look at the board').
Look carefully at the shape of these ammonite fossils and imagine them lying on the bottom of the sea (engages imagination).
Listen to this sentence/story and see if you can pick out ... (specific items).
Feet firmly on the floor and looking this way.
All eyes on the top of the board now, please.
David, tell me what you think ... (specific student directive).
Why do you think he's right, Sharon? (specific student question).

Once the penny drops about directive language, you will observe experienced teachers using it as a way to focus attention. Directive language signals how a teacher wants the students to focus. Some directions are loaded with expectations, such as 'All eyes on Question 3 because I'm going to ask one of you to answer.' Not only does the class have to find Question 3, but they know they have to read it and answer. When you hear good teacher-talk from colleagues you will begin to hone those phrases and scripts. Teacher-talk is not difficult to learn, but making it second nature needs a good deal of practice.

Classrooms are full of good positive starts, many of which lead nowhere. As a trainee your one thought may be just to survive until the end of a lesson. This is almost impossible if you do not think about what comes next, something which seems so obvious it is hard to imagine you would forget it.

How to invite poor behaviour

- Your teaching lacks pace and structure.
- Your lesson content does not match the age and ability of students (the work is too easy/too hard and boring).
- You rarely give praise.
- There are inadequate routines.
- You have a routine but do not stick to it (e.g. students putting up their hands).
- You become diverted too easily by children's well-meaning interruptions.
- You fail to set a task and verify that a child understands and has started it.
- Your objectives exist but lack emphasis on what you are looking for particularly in the students' work.
- There is poor scanning of the classroom to check for problems.
- You spend too long on the introduction, resulting in bored students.
- You are poor at monitoring on-task behaviour.
- You do not set deadlines and make your objectives clear to students.
- An activity takes too long (no variety).
- You ignore students who are not working.

Scripting for self-discipline

Children try to use their teacher as a trouble-fixer, so are often keen to tell tales about each other. The difficulty with this is that some of the tales are justified and some are not. One way to deal with tell-tales is simply to say, 'Thank you for telling me' and ignore them. Another is to have a tell-tale box and get them to write down the problem to be looked at later. One teacher I know only ever dealt with tale-telling during breaktime, depriving the whole class of their recreation time. This soon put a stop to telling tales. Yet another and far better approach is to have a system of 'talking-out', where the injured parties have to make some attempt to resolve problems themselves. Some students bully others with name-calling and insults, so the tale-telling about bullying is justified and has to be addressed. Other tale-telling is for rule infringement, which of course seems unfair to the students who follow class rules.

Responses to tale-telling

Are you telling me this to get someone into trouble?
Why are you telling me?
Write it down and put it in the box.
Maybe they're doing that because they don't know how to behave yet. But you do.
Yes. We have rules, but they're not as good as behaving well because we *want* to.
Is this a 'tell-tale' or something really serious?

Tale-telling is an irritating intrusion into teaching. You cannot ignore what is said entirely because there may be bullying going on and you will have to deal with that. Some students are very dependent attention-seekers – their tale-telling is part of their dependency. They appear as if from nowhere and behave like your shadow, following you everywhere. Ultimately you are trying to make them independent students who can take a few decisions without being prompted. The simple way forward may be to state honestly: 'You need to learn to work by yourself without asking me so often.' Also, you may need to explain the difference between telling tales and telling to inform about danger. Your inexperienced response to tale-telling may be unfair if you are starting out on a teaching career. This is just a fact of life, the alternative being plagued by tales of woe you are expected to handle.

Scripting for self-discipline is essentially a matter of devising phrases that trigger reminders and make students think. The shortest reminder is actually to say 'Think!' as you pass by a student. They have no idea why you have said it, but seem to refocus their attention anyway. Who knows? They may be thinking about that other scripted phrase you honed: 'What are you doing that I don't like?' or its neighbour, 'What are you doing that you shouldn't be doing?'

Questions for reflection

- What is my experience so far of saying things the wrong way round?
- What do I want to achieve in my teacher-talk?
- How would I adapt the script in this chapter for younger children?
- Why is eye-contact and specific direction so important?
- What routines will need consistent teacher-talk?
- What do I already do that I could shorten to a signal?
- What is the difference between using signals that are heard and those that are seen?
- What signals have I observed colleagues using with their students?

Checklist summary

- Say what you need and want, not what you don't.
- Alternate between control statements such as 'I expect politeness and concentration' and work statements such as 'Hands up who can tell me . . . '
- In the initial stages of your attention-getting strategy, stop all questions, stand still and stick to the script.
- No script is going to fit every occasion because you are working with students, not robots.
- Requests to remember, imagine, sort out, improve or change demand much more of students.
- Avoid nagging for self-discipline as this contradicts what you want to achieve.
- Preface with 'When you are working with me . . .' to establish routines.
- Experienced teachers are able to return to a positive sound in their voice almost immediately as if a switch has been thrown.
- Many things that teachers say can be shortened to signals.

4 Prevention and cure

I've told him, he needs to be firmer in the afternoons because they're more difficult. He's a trainee teacher who hasn't quite grasped that yet, so they mess about a bit. Then he gets angry, which is a big mistake.

(Supervising teacher-mentor, Year 5)

What does it mean to be firm but fair?

You may wonder why experienced teachers can seem rather hard on their students yet still retain a sense of humour and positivity. They know that if they deal with small problems early, they will have fewer serious difficulties later on. As soon as you possibly can, develop a teaching style where you are active rather than passive, determined and quietly insistent rather than patiently tolerant of poor behaviour. When trainees are given the usual advice 'Be firm, but fair', there are no real indicators of what this means. One teacher's idea of being firm is another's idea of bossiness. Maybe you want to be nice as a good role model for your class. However, teachers in their first year of a full-time post often wish that they had been firmer at the beginning of the year. Children test limits, so you need a good idea of what being firm actually means. If you want to create a good working relationship there are steps along the way to professionalism that will probably go against your instinct.

Three ways to deal with misbehaviour

There are three main ways of tackling students who behave as you would not like them to:

- distraction;
- conduct reminders;
- consequences.

(Continued)

First, you can remind students about work targets to distract them. Second, you can refer to infringement of behaviour codes and the student's responsibility for conduct. Third, there are consequences for not responding to the first two.

It is a mistake to see firmness as being in any way military and enforcing, because that can be counterproductive. An authoritarian formal approach is likely to make students clam up and not offer much. Sometimes you can roll forward the activities that students will do, striking a balance between formality and your determination to succeed. You can be tolerant but absolutely determined that you will involve the class by contrasting enthusiastic teaching and mid-sentence pauses to regain attention. If you have any intuition, you will plan a variety of activities more appropriate to a reduced afternoon's concentration level. Having said that, remember that a skilful teacher can still generate concentration last thing on a Friday afternoon. If you are very good at moving forward with enthusiasm, pausing occasionally but being tolerant, you will get more from students because they feel comfortable rather than threatened. In the heat of the moment, you can be forgiven for sliding into negativity, but you still need to pull back from that granite-faced look to remain rewarding.

Being firm with students can be demonstrated with a click of your fingers. Skilful trainee teachers can notice a student who is not paying attention and not even look at them. Like lightning they click their fingers and point at the student without eye-contact. The click is a message, but its effectiveness depends on how quickly peripheral vision picks up the non-attention. You might need to alternate this with the more conventional tactic of using a student's name, or click and name at the same time. Students tend to mimic an overused strategy, so a firm 'Sophie!' may be your specific message within a mid-sentence pause. The timing of what you say is what marks you out as firm, and it is better to do this sooner rather than later.

> I've learned to stop the lesson dead in its tracks when anyone drifts or chatters at the start of my explanation. They know now that if I stop twice, I put a figure one on the board. If I have to stop again, I add a tick meaning a minute's lost breaktime and they have to prove they have worked hard enough for it to be cancelled. After that it's changed to a two, three or four-minute loss. I started out by warning and threatening, but I've found actually it's better to demonstrate it. They soon get the message. (Trainee teacher)

Firm behaviour management is never supposed to be a battleground. If you want to win battles, choose another profession, because turning teaching into a war is not a good way to avoid stress. Your firmness is sometimes a statement made to a difficult child rather than a battle won. You cannot make students do anything they refuse to do, only persuade them they should think about the consequences if they do not. If you let them know that you disapprove, as in 'You need to think about acceptable behaviour and what happens if you don't do that', at least you have stated your firmness. There is no guarantee that students will change direction, but at least their behaviour was registered.

Being firm is frequently demonstrated at the start of a lesson. That is when, apart from gaining attention, you check for all sorts of minor irritants such as chewing gum addicts and hat-wearers. The way you are firm spells out the kind of teacher that you are. You could confront, but a better way would be 'Craig, you can chew but not in the classroom, thanks', 'No sliding under the desk, thanks Bethany'. Firmness means you get the physical organization as you want it: 'Beth, chair turned facing this way please, and Leon too please, so we can start.' Trainees who are sloppy about these details invite problems because they do not establish the difference between when to listen, when to discuss, when to pay attention and when to work on your own. They blur these distinctions.

Refusing to be hooked by the bait

It is too easy to say 'Ignore the bad behaviour and praise the good' because not everything students do can be ignored. Sometimes you can distract them instead of confront them, a process of involving students in work by directing their attention towards what you want. You can say 'Kylie, I know this is difficult, but you're coping *very* well.' Follow this with 'Look at that sentence carefully because I'll need to ask you a question in a couple of minutes.' If Kylie continues to be difficult, you are thrown back on class codes of behaviour. Provided, that is, they were set up well in the first place. You have to have codes of conduct and procedures that are points of referral or there is no basis for letting students know what is reasonable and acceptable. Sometimes these may be listed as rules because young children seem to understand them better than more global behaviour codes, such as 'being polite' or 'treating each other with respect'.

Ignoring bad behaviour is possible but difficult and you will need to use your judgement about when to do this. If you ignore bad behaviour it sends out a powerful signal – it gives the message that the behaviour gets no reward. Students often misbehave to see if you will take the bait, in which case they win because they gain your attention or because it invites a power struggle that they can enjoy. For ignoring to be a successful and powerful signal there has to be plenty of praise continually given elsewhere. The idea of giving plenty of praise elsewhere is that the malcontents in the class will actually want some of it. Better still, if you can genuinely praise something that a difficult child does, you may be able to divert them, as in: 'Well done Simon for getting ready! We just need you listening with no extra talking now.'

How you say this can influence what happens. You want to send out the message that students will get attention for cooperating and will be ignored when they do not. In Chapter 1, using a voice tone as calm as reading a telephone directory was recommended when dealing with bad behaviour. The advice was to save your emotional energy for positive praise, and make sure that your calm 'telephone directory' voice was not sounding weary or bored. Voice tone is not something that you can learn from a book, so my suggestion is that you use a purposeful, calm but clear public voice. This will vary slightly depending on the age group that you are teaching, especially if it is a reception class. Returning to this theme, there are some general guidelines. You do not want to sound as if you have endless patience and will wait for ever (calm but passive). Neither do you want to sound annoyed (calm but obviously just about to explode). Nor do you want to sound uninterested or unapproachable (wake me up when my pay cheque arrives). Occasionally – possibly rarely – frustration will get the better of you and you will sound angry. There is actually nothing wrong with sounding human and showing your negative feelings once in a while. Why would you always want to hide your anger? Teachers are not saints and students need to see that for themselves.

Teachers who are poor at managing their class shout much more frequently at students and use anger as the main but misguided means of class control. It is far better to sound as if you are very much in control of yourself and keen to move the lesson forwards as positively as you can. Control yourself in a crisis before you control the class. Remember that outer wall of your stomach (see Chapter 2). During those first few moments of gaining attention, or even when you want to refocus attention, you can occasionally use a very strong and loud 'No!' when there is too much chatter. This needs to be done immediately there is too much chatter, not left as a last resort. Follow it with a pause and calmly but firmly add whatever you need to persist in refocusing attention. An assertive teacher does not wait forever. Problems arise when a loud 'No!' becomes a bad habit. Once you diminish the effect of your 'No!' by overuse, out will come a fresh idea to bait you and see if you respond.

What is in the voice this time? You do not want to fuel a difficult situation. In 2005, the *Times Educational Supplement* 'First Appointments' section ran a cartoon by John Fardell. It depicted classroom gerbils in a cage as 'People Who Know More About Teaching Than You Do' and the angry exchange went like this:

Teacher: Liam! Get back to your table!
Gerbils: She's really struggling with discipline, this one . . .
Teacher: Liam, put the staple gun down! Come on, I'll let you play on the computer . . .
Gerbils: Classic mistake! Never reward bad behaviour . . .
Teacher: Liam, you LITTLE SOD! Give me the staple gun or I'll throttle you!
Gerbils: Ooh, she shouldn't have said that. She'll lose the whole class now.

Although this scene is exaggerated, there are several important messages for beginners. Apart from rewarding bad behaviour, the teacher's other mistake is attempting to strike a bargain with Liam. Never bargain with students. The teacher who says 'Behave well and I'll let you go on the computer' is asking for trouble. Worse still, the teacher who agrees to a child who says 'I'll finish this Miss if you let me go on the computer' has forgotten who is supposed to be in charge. There is nothing wrong with rewards, so long as they are not turned into bribes with which to strike bargains. Students quickly understand that by behaving in certain ways they may be rewarded, but that is quite different. They also sense that shouting means that the teacher is less in control of themselves. Liam's teacher could handle this script better. Imagine you are Liam's teacher and you first shout 'Liam!', then drop your voice slightly. The temptation when Liam does not respond first time is to raise the pitch and volume of your voice. Do the opposite:

> Teacher: Liam! [*Liam takes no notice*] Liam. [*still takes no notice, teacher pauses*] Liam.
> Liam: What? [*turns round with staple gun in his hand*]
> Teacher: [*lowers voice to calm assertive speaking volume*] Back to your table please and leave the staple gun there. I'll come and look at your work in a second.

There is no guarantee that Liam will go back to his table or that he will put down the staple gun. If he does not move, the classic remedy is to offer him a choice that he will not like. He needs time to move, but if he refuses you can say something along the lines of 'Liam, you can move now, or you'll have to stay at the end of the lesson and explain why. Up to you.' Liam will probably move back reluctantly, but give him plenty of time. Notice that the teacher in this improved exchange says nothing to Liam until she is sure she has his attention. She ignores Liam's impolite 'What?' because dealing with this is not the main concern that she has. If Liam refuses to give attention after hearing his name three times, the teacher cuts to the chase and says 'Liam. We'll need to discuss this later and there will be consequences.' The threat of deferred consequences is real but not specific, leaving Liam to imagine all sorts of things. Instead of a confrontation and ongoing argument the teacher leaves Liam alone, but he has not won the battle. He still has the threat of possible punishment hanging over him. Given an opportunity to avoid further explanation without the benefit of his usual audience, most likely he will settle down to some work. He will prefer to live now rather than pay later.

Some students are brilliant at seeking attention and hooking you in – they do this either by making remarks or actually doing something that annoys you. For example, you might refuse to take the bait if you receive a cheeky reply to your question 'What are you doing, Peter?' The reply from Peter might be 'Dunno. What's it look like I'm doin'?', which is an open invitation to react negatively to his annoying response. The best tactic is to describe what you see as I described in the previous chapter. 'Looks like you're talking a lot and not working . . .', 'Looks like you're out of your seat finding somebody to interrupt . . .', 'Looks like you find it hard to concentrate' or 'Looks like you haven't started working yet.' Peter might reply with excuses such as: 'I'm just starting', 'I'm borrowing a pencil off Jason', or 'I'm already working! You're always picking on me!' This could be to see whether you will be hooked into an argument. Your response still needs to be the famous one-liner: 'What should you be doing?' repeated several times without extra chat.

You might be offered the bait twice, maybe three times, but you must return to your one-liner. The best response to a further attempt to bait you, such as 'You can *see* I'm just getting a pencil!' is either to repeat 'What should you be doing by now?', or if Peter wants to keep up his smart replies, stop asking a question and *tell* him: 'You need to be working Peter, and I can't see that yet.' Some students want the last word, so they mutter under their breath, or mimic 'You need to be working, nah nah ne nah nah'. Although this technically counts as cheek, you can ignore it for the time being. If you hear mimicry such as 'You need to be working and I can't see that yet', you can always laugh, and say 'Quite right!' as you turn away. You refuse to be manipulated. As a tactic it has these four basic steps, including the final strategy of stating your case and walking away.

1   Ask the student what they are doing.
2   Expect the attempt to bait you, but respond by *describing* what you see that needs changing.
3   Ask what the student *should* be doing.
4   If there is no satisfactory reply, *describe* what you need the student to do. Make this your one-liner and just repeat it. Turn your back and walk away.

One further low-level way in which students disrupt is to pretend that they are helpless, sidetracking teachers into helping them. This is sometimes quite subtle and consequently it needs astute handling. It may not appear to be disruptive, but what follows this helplessness certainly can be. A small core of students give up easily and over time learn that there are rewards for being helpless and needy. As a beginner it is easy to be sucked into pleas for help that are actually pleas for attention, leading to a general disruption of the task. Children are very clever at working out what will get them the most attention and giving up quickly is just one of their tactics. After a whole-class introduction that you know is clear, one you have verified before setting a task, students often need to work independently for as long as possible. Pleas for help can be resisted with 'You're working well. Carry on and I'll look again in a few minutes.' As you can imagine, this requires good judgement on your part. Students might genuinely need your help so you have to be able to spot the difference between faked helplessness and the real thing. There is nothing wrong with the expectation that students will try their best without needing help for at least five minutes. Beyond the five minutes, help needs to be provided but never so readily that students stop thinking for themselves. If you prevent them from demanding early attention, you also prevent disruption.

Follow this up with reminders about codes of behaviour for listening or working at a task. Instructions such as 'We all need to keep both feet on the floor' fit any age. Younger children can cope with 'Everyone's back needs to be straight so we can all concentrate'. These are physical reminders of readiness to work. They may smack of Victorian drill but they have a good track record. Older children may have difficulty with the idea of sitting up straight, partly because they have experienced it so much at a younger age. Saying 'I don't want you looking like soldiers on parade, but I do need you all concentrating' may be your alternative. If in doubt, reinforce codes of behaviour. This is especially important if you have several low-level disrupters. Without a clear code reinforced, it is very difficult to appeal to the rest of the class.

Switching the focus to the positive behaviour of the whole class can change agreed rules into good habits. How students sit is not exactly a rule, but it stems from the general expectation that they will be ready to learn. You can praise students for what they are doing that emphasizes the good work happening. You can praise students who show that they are ready and those who remember those six or seven 'readiness' items of which you hoped you never needed to remind them. You can praise students who are concentrating on their work. You can praise effort as well as achievement.

Not everything regarding low-level disruption needs punitive action. There is an ancient Chinese saying that sums up many difficult situations: 'Muddy water, if left alone, will clear by itself.' I think I would change that slightly for a beginner teacher: 'Muddy water, if left alone, will *sometimes* clear by itself.' If you deliberately choose to ignore certain facets of behaviour, this is not the same as taking no action whatsoever. The water clears itself because you recognize what is happening and make a decision to leave it alone. You are not passive about this because you move on quickly and distract students, much as was described in Chapter 2 – gaining attention without waiting forever.

Positive prevention through class rules and targets

When facing a new class, experienced teachers rarely pin a list of rules to the wall in their first lesson. This is because the ability to manage a class is actually demonstrated from minute to minute. You may need some rules, but you will fare better if first you involve students in an enjoyable task with clear directions about what you want. Rules can wait. The reason that they need demonstrating is because students forget them from moment to moment anyway. Stop the class if its conduct does not match expectations, and refer to acceptable codes of behaviour. There will be routines about going to the toilet. You may have a rule about when students are legitimately out of their seats and a code of behaviour for how they behave when they are in their seats. There will be rules for what happens when students are late. There may be rules about school uniform and PE kit. There may be expectations about homework or behaviour on school trips.

Rules can invite students to break them, which is why they need to be few in number and eventually refer to responsibilities. Points of reference, such as class rules and targets, are set up so that both you and the students that you teach understand what is agreed. Rules and routines are useful for everyone; they are there so you can quote them without getting personal or confrontational. You refer to rules when students are not involved in work, are off-task or socially irresponsible. They are your reference only when learning targets fail.

Targets can divert attention away from quoting rules because they focus on learning and away from bad behaviour. Specific learning targets, such as 'Finding the vocabulary for our work on pollution', or 'Using scissors accurately to cut the card for our models' give you reference points for praising work. I prefer work targets and effort targets accompanied by deadlines to rules any day. Rules can be quoted all over the place, but targets can refer specifically to achievement, motivation and progress. The way that targets function is that they are put into teaching plans on a daily basis to emphasize what the teacher will be looking for. These sharpen the focus of activity and involve students in a common cause. You can quote targets by saying 'John, you're forgetting that we're trying to prove we can subtract large numbers accurately', or 'Abigail, remember our target for improving the writing.' Class targets could be summarized as: 'What We are Trying to Achieve' (WWTA). Unfortunately the acronym WWTA does not work so well as the familiar WILF (What I am Looking For) because it is not someone's name. WILF sits better on the tongue than WWTA, but it invites students to please the teacher rather than acts as a class target. This may seem to be a subtlety. Perhaps pleasing the teacher is not the worst that a child can do if it means that they make progress. I much prefer a more cooperative WWTA, but WILF will do for the present.

Looking for a target, something in particular to achieve in a task, is not exactly revolutionary. An internet search for WILF using Google (www. google.co.uk) reveals examples from almost every corner of the land, including official local education authority sites. Targets are simply there to give emphasis and points of reference in your teaching. If you decide to search the internet you will find enough examples to give you an idea of how to devise your own. Only a few of the internet examples you find will be useful as ready-made targets to inject quality into tasks. Most will fit other people's lessons, not yours. Lessons need very specific targets. Sharing WILF objectives and quality targets with students is essential. If all you ever do is look for things to evaluate your teaching, you miss the point. When teachers say 'What I am looking for is important examples of recycling for us to discuss', or 'What I am looking for is accuracy in measuring the square of paper', these are shared quality targets. They also contrast with the most common targets, such as neatness, task-completion or the number of answers completed in a worksheet. If you have a quality WILF that looks for 'How well you can explain the way energy is generated by a wind turbine' the implication is that you will focus on children's ability to explain.

Once you have built targets into your planning, you have the perfect opportunity to refer to them positively. If you never set anything up in the first place, your praise will be general rather than specific. You will find it hard to praise without resorting to the shorthand of 'Brilliant effort!', or a global 'Fantastic!' as praise. You cannot say anything as specific as 'Well done Emily! I can see that you set out your maths problem accurately and have thought about subtracting large numbers', or 'That's a fantastic effort you've made Darren, to cooperate with sharing equipment in your group. Well done!' In WILF terms, the targets are 'We are looking for people who can share in a group' and 'We are looking to see how well we set out the maths problem.' Your praise inflates the bank balance of positive encouragement and sets the tone for moving students forward in their learning. Targets help you to develop a positive running commentary as you go around the room describing what you see. You can be observant and positive down to the last detail.

The immediacy of specific learning targets allows you quite justifiably to question a child who has gone off-task or lost focus, asking: 'What are we trying to achieve here?' Reception class children may not understand the word 'achieve', so it might be: 'What are we trying to learn?' or 'What are we trying to do?' Even 'What's our magic wish for this work?' can be appropriate. Your reference point makes it much easier to question as well as praise students. Consequently, it is worth spending some time setting up the specific desirable features of your lesson, apart from the usual need for concentration, accuracy, checking for errors, clear layout. Try saying, for example, 'I'm looking for those of you who can . . .' then specifically praise what you find. In this way you reinforce the target and stand a better chance of bringing students back on track if they drift.

Class rules need to be simple reference points or they are soon ignored. If you decide to set up a discussion to agree rules, you may find that unnecessary rules emerge. Instead of 'Speak politely' you may be offered 'No swearing in class', which is negative and not necessary. Rules need to have consequences attached or they are worthless.

Rules

- Look and listen to talker
- Follow instructions carefully
- Treat others as we would like to be treated
- Move carefully and quietly in class
- Keep our hands and feet to ourselves
- Respect our own and others' property

(Continued)

Consequences

- Warning
- Isolation
- Lost play or lunchtime
- Detention
- See headteacher
- Contact parents

You could have negative rules such as: no talking when I do; no hitting; no rudeness; no running in the classroom; no touching anyone else; and no destruction of property. But this is like coming into the classroom with all guns blazing. There is nothing that tells students what to do, only what they should not do. The rules are reasonable because they describe a positive code of social behaviour. There is nothing there that says 'Don't do this'. If rules are negative, the chances are that they will generate a climate of negative comments from you as a teacher. They set a tone of negativity which can be pervasive. Inevitably, the outcome will be unrewarding for the whole class. In addition, there will be an enormous vacuum still to be filled regarding what you want students to do when they have stopped doing whatever the rule told them to do. Behaving according to positive codes is a fundamental principle of good class rules. However obvious you think this is, count up the number of times you tell students not to do things. We are all human, so naturally there will be a margin of error. The trouble is that it is easy to slip into negativity in all sorts of subtle ways and escalate behaviour problems without realizing why this is happening.

Usually, adding reasons will help to reinforce the 'do's' and 'don'ts' of classroom rules. Two examples are: 'We keep our hands and feet to ourselves *because* we all need to work safely, not interrupted by anyone else'; and 'Keep water off the floor *because* someone may slip.' It is not always possible to think on your feet and give a reason, but codes of conduct driven by good reasons are more likely to be accepted. Some reasons can be given an outing during a session about health and safety. Others will have a history, such as 'We walk around the school *because* there have been nasty accidents in the past when people ran.' Reasons can encourage a culture which does not depend on having rules for the sake of it.

Naturally, without rules you cannot say 'You're choosing not to follow our rules about speaking when you shouldn't'. If the rule is agreed by the class you claim no personal responsibility for its existence; the rule is for the whole class or part of the wider school behaviour code. This distances you from anything personal and is a common device used in societies throughout the world. Its main characteristic is that it refers to a third party or distant authority. Universities refer to external examiners and regulations. The police refer to the law. Military units refer to queen's or king's regulations and teachers refer to school rules.

The rule states, for example, 'No student will swing back on a chair.' Ask yourself if you ever swung back on a chair at school. There is that wonderfully enjoyable moment when you wonder if this time you can balance for a few seconds longer. Will the chair tip backwards? Can I support the chair by holding on to my desk and appearing to hover? Am I going backwards or forwards and how do I make that tiny adjustment to balance again? In the 1930s a teacher would not have needed to have any rule about swinging back on a chair because seats were fixed to the desk, sometimes to the floor as well. I am not recommending a return to those days, but your expectations and rules will arise as much from physical organization as the social dynamic. Is there an expectation that students will arrive with their own pen and pencil? Do they have responsibility for the way that they borrow and lend equipment, such as scissors or erasers? Is there any understanding about students' responsibility for sharing equipment? At the social level, what conventions are there for discussing work in a group?

Whatever rules you establish, you can be sure that they exist within the context of your teaching style, the school itself and the ethos created by the headteacher and staff. It is not just that some students behave worse than others. Some schools are better run and some teachers are more skilful at handling difficult students. I have visited hundreds of schools in my career. The atmosphere and behaviour of students seems to have more to do with agreed wholeschool codes of conduct than the successes of a few dedicated teachers. A settled school environment affects how staff work, and headteachers would probably be the first to admit that they did not achieve this by imposing a set of rigid rules. Your concern from day-to-day will be survival in the classroom, but do not be surprised if you need to learn about the established school aspirations, expectations and routines. You cannot work in isolation, even though you will need to handle most situations in the classroom yourself.

Once put into practice, agreed rules can become the foundation for self-discipline. Consequences for breaking these are really a 'stepped' discipline policy for dealing with students. Whatever consequences you decide, these have to be part of a whole school policy. You cannot go out on a limb and invent your own if they conflict with a school's agreed approach. Several additional routines may be necessary, but some of these can be understood as class habits under the rule that says: 'Treat others as we would like to be treated.' This particular rule does not mean a great deal because it is wide open to interpretation, so you will need to establish additional routines. Putting a hand up to speak is more a learned routine than a rule. Routines for sorting out equipment and looking after it are important, as are agreed routines for coming in and out of the classroom. Most teachers can manage 'Hands up, who can tell me ...', but this ritual can become embedded so that 'Hands up' does not need saying if everyone understands that there should be no calling out.

Some very difficult students follow the rules of other students rather than the established class rules. Peer-group pressure is always a strong feature of school life. They may fear reprisals from classmates or bullying may be happening. They may be involved with the police outside of the school day and not want to follow any codes of conduct except their own. Most likely a new teacher would find that these students are already on a personal behaviour plan, reporting to a member of staff higher up the chain of school discipline. If you came into teaching wide-eyed and innocent, you could find it hard to understand that some students quite genuinely draw little distinction between right and wrong. Rules are understood by the majority of students, but not all. As has been said elsewhere, some students are so self-absorbed that the idea that they should take notice of rules does not occur to them.

Transforming rules into responsibilities

Teachers often use rules as reminders when they refer to them. 'David, remember our rule about sharing please' emphasizes a class rule but may not persuade David to behave responsibly. David might need to be reminded constantly because there is no real reason why he should remember. Perhaps he has very few social skills so rules do not mean much, and he forgets them anyway. You could have a rule that nobody speaks at the same time as you, but do you need one? If it is a class rule, you stand a better chance of enforcing it but you have not yet handed over responsibility for listening. In Chapter 1, it was suggested that your longer-term aim is to encourage self-discipline. Doing this successfully involves you in a gradual process of abandoning rules and handing over responsibility. This does not mean that you create a class full of little parrots who continually shout out the rules themselves. It means that there is some subtle teacher-talk to learn. Here are some contrasting examples in which it is not being suggested that rules are unnecessary, simply that there is more value in self-responsibility.

Referring to the rule:	'Remember our rule about not shouting.'
Referring to responsibility:	'Peter. You're able to use your voice better than that so we can all concentrate.'
Referring to the rule:	'Darren, remember our rule about not stopping anyone else working.'
Referring to responsibility:	'Darren, you're quite responsible enough to do this by yourself, so let Peter get on with his work too.'
Referring to the rule:	'Kim, remember we keep our hands and feet to ourselves.'
Referring to responsibility:	'Kim, it's up to you to sit there without bothering anyone else.'
Referring to the rule:	'Remember our rule about litter off the floor.'

Referring to responsibility:	'When the room's looking OK to leave, we'll do that.'
Referring to the rule:	'Ben. You've forgotten the rule about being out of your seat.'
Referring to responsibility:	'Ben, tell me why you're not working.'

Notice the inclusion of 'When . . . then' (which was mentioned in Chapter 3). This time it is not 'When you . . .' but effectively 'When the room is looking OK, *then* we can leave', inviting group responsibility. For this to happen, you would need to have made it quite clear on previous occasions that it did not matter so much who dropped the litter, but that it was everyone's responsibility to tidy the room before leaving it.

Early years teachers need a slightly different set of examples. The following are from a reception class teacher, working in a difficult city area.

Referring to the rule:	'Sophie, what are you doing climbing in the water tray? We've washed the floor already today. Remember: the rule is, feet on the ground!'
Referring to responsibility:	'Sophie, if you climb in the water tray and it tips over, you will have to spend the rest of your playtime mopping the floor!'
Referring to the rule:	'Look at those filthy pillows! The rule is heads on pillows, feet on floor!'
Referring to responsibility:	'Curtis, if you want to jump on the cushions with dirty feet, you will need to wash the covers afterwards.'
Referring to the rule:	'For heaven's sake keep still, will you! The rule is, we sit still and listen on the carpet.'
Referring to responsibility:	'Freya, your bottom is very fidgety today ... it needs to remember to be still so that the other students are not disturbed.'
Referring to the rule:	'Leon, remember we look after our toys!'
Referring to responsibility:	'Leon, if those toys are broken when you have finished throwing them, you will need to mend them for playtime tomorrow.'

Prevention as a resource issue

Many behavioural problems can be prevented by remembering and anticipating the resources needed to teach. Nothing new there, you might think, but if you are starting out on your career this requires some thought. There are a few obvious issues, such as whether students need the same resources at exactly the same moment. This is something you try to avoid, which is why there are enough scissors, paper and so on for the class. You need to overplan your resources, leaving nothing to chance.

My teacher has a 'Helper Box' on each group table. This is a box file containing a dictionary, a couple of rulers, a pair of scissors, an eraser, two spare pencils, a number square to 100 and a list of commonly known difficult spellings. It saves no end of time and frustration. (Trainee teacher)

Some teachers have racks for almost everything. The reason for this is to run a resource system where the rack is always full. Having brushes, scissors, even pencils in a rack means that they can be searched for without counting at the end of the day or the end of a practical session. Otherwise there are your secret monitors to do the counting. More advanced resources are necessary for subjects such as design technology and science. Students cannot saw wood if there are not enough saws or bench-hooks and science makes similar demands for enough equipment. The prevention actually fades into the background once you discover how smoothly lessons can go if they are well resourced. There are fewer frustrations and fewer students left queuing for equipment.

Finally, prevention through good resourcing includes checking whether those resources actually work. Science sessions can be ruined because bulbs and batteries fail. Computer suites are relatively reliable, but can still fail. You may not manage to do anything about computer failure, but you can do something about the provision of glue, fasteners, tape and other teaching resources. Traditionally, prevention is better than cure. You may think that this chapter is full of good ideas that work, but the underlying message is that quite mundane resourcing and managing is necessary to prevent problems arising in the first place.

Questions for reflection

- Why do rules need consequences?
- How important are good resources in preventing trouble?
- What alternatives are there to continually resetting noise levels?
- Why does keeping hands and feet to ourselves prevent problems?
- Why do rules need to be few in number and agreed by the class?
- When does behaviour management become a battle?

Checklist summary

- There are three ways to deal with misbehaviour: distraction, conduct reminders and consequences. First, refer the students back to work. Second, refer to infringement of rules. Third, give consequences for ignoring distraction and conduct reminders.
- Control yourself in a crisis before you control the class.
- 'Muddy water, if left alone, will *sometimes* clear by itself.'
- Never bargain with students.
- Make sure you have a culprit's attention before you direct them to do something.
- If you haven't set anything up in the first place, your praise will be general rather than specific.

- If you stand firm, the routine will happen. If you give way and blur the routine, it will fail.
- Rules set clear boundaries of agreed social behaviour.
- Say 'You can' and defer it with 'when'.
- You distract, assert yourself, or impose consequences.
- Prevent problems by thinking carefully about the resources needed.

5 Noise levels, voice tone and more teacher-talk

The dreaded 'Shhh . . .'

Continually 'Shhh-ing' a class is a waste of breath. The noise level comes down for a few seconds, but rises because there is nothing to fill the vacuum. Replace 'Shhh' with what you really want. It is not just that you want less noise. You do, but this needs expressing as a requirement for concentration, attention to detail, brain-power and independent thought. State what you want, rather than what you do not.

Stating what you want

'Use your whisper voices please.'
'Do your talking inside your head, please.'
'Eyes, ears and mouth as they are supposed to be, please!'
'Need you concentrating so I can think too.'
'Need you thinking about the detail.'
'Think about how well this needs to be done.'

Noise is a precursor to disruption, but a silent classroom is not necessarily the best atmosphere for learning. In earlier chapters it was suggested that you describe what you see. In the case of noisy classes, this is more difficult because you need to be heard over the noise level to make your point in the first place. Teachers tend to revert to raising their voices and saying things such as 'We can't start with this noise', or they stop a class to regain the focus of attention. If you stop a class this gives you the chance to describe what you see, giving a catalogue of minor instances of inattention, and say what you want. Most likely you want concentration and will use the well-tried device of describing what this looks like (variations on 'I want to see heads in books, pens working, feet on the floor, a good writing position and mouths closed').

Noise abatement needs persistence, setting and resetting noise levels until you hope you can sense an atmosphere of concentration. This is the opposite of what happens to a pantomime audience. Buttons (of Cinderella fame) tries to train the audience to shout louder, shouting 'That's not loud enough', repeating this until it is. When you set noise levels, you need to interrupt within a nanosecond several times until the level is as low as you want it.

Some students are so needy that noise is natural to them and you will rarely achieve a quiet atmosphere. This does not mean that they cannot learn. You might prefer peace and quiet, but remember that some students do not feel comfortable unless they are surrounded by noise. There are definitely some students who need to talk out their thoughts to learn, just as there are more introspective students who want to think things through. One of your best tactics is to focus attention on the task strongly enough for noise to subside, but you will still need to set the noise level because noise generally escalates. Students compete to hear one another and this leads to louder voices being used (which is why a 'No calling across the room' rule is sometimes necessary).

Non-verbal disturbance

What do you do if there is annoying non-verbal behaviour such as a noisy twanging ruler, or a difficult child decides to prod another student? What if a younger child is trying to hinder another one on the carpeted area by gesturing, flicking an ear or smoothing their hair? What if a student decides to make stupid noises or whistle? You do not want to reward bad behaviour, so do you ignore it? Recognize that noises are one of the easiest ways to disrupt, and will be more frequent only if you do not take action. Noises still have to be handled, so dealing with an individual may be necessary, such as 'Bethany. You're not working with the rest of us and I need to keep an eye on that. I'll look again at your work in a couple of minutes.' Situations may need to be put on a backburner, as in: 'Dylan, we'll need to talk about this later. Better get on with your work for the moment.' Alternatively, there are ways to keep individuals out of the equation yet let them 'know that you know that *they* know that *you* know'. You will have seen this at school yourself when teachers pretend not to have spotted the culprits and issue a global warning instead. Usually this takes the form of signalling that the behaviour is not acceptable to the whole class. '*Someone* is making silly noises and that has to stop' (Miss, it's Liam again!), or 'We keep our hands and feet to ourselves and not everybody has remembered that.' Keeping negative comments in the third person, a teacher can say almost anything without attacking an individual.

There is a sleight of hand involved when you say '*Someone* in the class isn't ready', 'We're not all ready', 'I can *still* hear someone making silly noises' or 'We don't make stupid noises in this class'. You appear not to know where the problem lies, but of course you do know who the culprit is and so do the students. Everyone is a conspirator to this familiar classroom game and most children will go along with it because they can avoid the glare of confrontation and the consequences of losing a battle of wills. Ultimately, you remain faced with a decision about whether to intervene directly, impose a sanction, give a warning or use your tally system (see Freya's tally chart in Chapter 3). The final decision is yours, because you know the relationship that you have with your students.

All misbehaviour has some purpose and the most difficult to deal with is behaviour intended to disrupt lessons without obviously doing so. Low-level disruption includes slightly 'over-busy' noises, furtive destruction such as minor sabotage of equipment needed for the lesson, or having a well-faked coughing fit. The intention is still to gain attention. If you overreact (rather than react) to this subversion there will be a power struggle. The pay-off will be that the peer group enjoys seeing their teacher on the run. You have lost. Students tend to like attention from their teachers, although their peers are also an obvious audience. Students who disrupt non-verbally without clear evidence probably think that they are good at stirring things up. They do it 'for a laugh', to get noticed. Occasionally students misbehave as a payback for being punished, but mostly their misbehaviour is driven by the need for attention and recognition. They fidget and are generally hyperactive just to be noticed frequently.

> There's this kid in my Year 6 who always has a forced sly grin on his face. He comes into the room as if he's already intending to be a comic vandal. The grin winds me up and it's as if everything he does is going to test my patience to the limit. This is all before he has actually done anything. I can see him looking for any chance he can get to entertain his mates. Sometimes he pretends to be helpful, but it's only part of his grin-filled attempt to set up another entertainment. (Year 6 teacher)

The insolent grin is legendary and needs to be ignored or deliberately misread, as in: 'I can see you look happy, so we'll need to build on that and work well together.' By saying the student looks happy you may have destroyed the insolent grin.

Noise and transitions

Most teachers have their ways of making a transition from one phase of the lesson to another. An example is the transition from an attention-getting explanation to the on-task phase of the lesson. If practical equipment is involved, there may be some noise of excitement as students begin to use it. Whenever you move to another phase of your teaching session, you are trying to clear the screen of the mind by pausing and regaining attention. You need to sound important and serious when you do this because you want students to treat things seriously too. Change your voice, and behave as if the next activity is completely different from what has been going on. If you were speaking slowly, speed up. If you were speaking quickly, slow down. Raise your voice, speak at a higher pitch of excitement or lower pitch of seriousness. In fact, do anything that contrasts with what went before. A good 'transition to task' is an opportunity to change your voice tone, refocus attention, clarify what the task is and give a reminder. You can finish with a 'When . . . then' command (see Chapter 3) such as 'When you go back to your desks', or 'When you've written the date . . .'.

Transitions are not too difficult to achieve if you have been following the scripting advice given in Chapter 3. Imagine that you have just explained a task that you want the students to do. If you were expecting a ready-made script at this point, try elaborating on this one. It comes into the category of summary reminders rather than a full-blown script:

> So . . . I've explained what your group is going to do. Remember, you're looking for better words to describe how Jason felt about being trapped in the van. When you get back to your places, find a pencil and immediately write down five useful adjectives to start.

Most students benefit from knowing what to do first when they begin a task. Besides a transition to the task, transitions occur at other times in a lesson. There is one at the end of a lesson and the beginning of another. There is also a transition from the end of the lesson to getting ready to leave the room for lunch. Transitions and changes of atmosphere sometimes need supporting with physical changes. Equipment may need to be given out or collected. Students may need to reorganize their workspace or line up at the door. You might want to move students to a different part of the room, ensuring that standing up and sitting down gives a new focus. Transitions are not just an irritating interlude between one work phase and another. They herald a new important phase of teaching and learning. It may be necessary to give instructions about *how* the students should move, as this is all part of making a good transition. You may need to regain the focus of attention, pausing as you shift your voice to another register or pace. There may be several 'We're not all ready' moments and scripting of a great deal of rather petty attention to detail, checking everyone has everything ready. In addition, you will need to reset the noise level if it has escalated.

Noise control routines are a frustration for many new teachers. Some classes use a noise monitor, which is a chart or gives responsibility to one student per group for keeping noise down. A strategy you may wish to try is to persist in establishing very clear 'settling time'. This is a short period when students legitimately make noise before 'concentration time'.

> I've found that when kids understand the difference between these two phases of a session you can say 'This is the time we do our talking inside our heads', or 'Settling time has finished.' You have to know that some activities . . . like collage are noisy. Others, like reading, are quiet. You won't achieve anything by complaining about the noise during

the first few minutes. Put a time limit on it and you'll let them know there is an end to the noise they make. Students need to be allowed time to sort themselves out and button their lips when it's time to do that. (Primary teacher)

Allowing settling time has close links with the idea mentioned in Chapter 1, where the on-task phase of the lesson prompted the teacher to say 'Just a moment, I'm checking first to see if everyone has started.' Sustained silence is rarely achievable, but concentration is. When students concentrate, the noise level will drop anyway.

Teacher-talk and coded messages

I visited a school a few years ago where the reception class only had to hear 'I'd like everyone on the carpeted area, please' to respond. As soon as their teacher said this, the children quietly walked over to the carpet, sat down facing her chair, eyes front, not talking or touching anyone else, with hands in their laps. Nothing else was said. The code meant that all this had been long-established (this is how we show we are ready when I ask you to sit on the carpet).

Short specific phrases within your script are often coded messages. You may remember any number of parental codes such as 'What time d'you call this?', 'Don't make me do this', 'I'm not interested in who started it', 'This hurts me more than it hurts you', and 'This is for your own good'. Teachers use coded messages too:

> Put your hand up if you're a packed lunch.
> I'm still waiting . . .
> Er . . . excuse me . . .
> Someone's being silly . . .
> Someone's asking to stay behind.
> There's still someone talking when I am.
> Sitting properly.

The more effective a coded message, the less intrusive and time-wasting it is going to be. There are coded messages, such as saying 'chair', meaning four chair legs on the floor, or 'quality', meaning almost anything connected with paying attention or concentrating. For these to work, you need to explain them first and test them. All that is needed is to tell students 'When I say "chair" it means that you sit with all four chair-legs on the floor.' You may decide that a signal for this is better than saying 'chair'. Some teachers would just click their fingers and point at the student. Once the code is established it becomes a useful shorthand. Some coded messages are individual, such as 'Liam. Writing!' which (for Liam) means he has to sit up to write, rather than write with his nose on the paper.

Good class, but will not stop talking

Maintaining a positive atmosphere when you are feeling annoyed is difficult. A recurrent problem in schools is that of a class that works hard but simply cannot stop chattering at inappropriate times. The following solution is more an effective last resort than a first-time solution, so needs using with caution – overuse will destroy its effect. It is appropriate for primary students, but take care to ensure that it does not become a way of life in your classroom:

> I've taken over this Year 5 class with a reputation for being chatterboxes. There's a very high proportion of boys and that might have something to do with it. I did all the usual stuff, like stopping every few seconds to get their attention back and sounding cross, impatient and disappointed. I've kept them back at break and I've given detentions. I really like this class because they're so enthusiastic and I don't want to get too negative with them. They're fantastic and we really get on well . . . In the end I decided to pick on chatterbox kids and make each of them stand up until they could be quiet. Soon I had three children standing when the rest of the class were sitting. The first day I had to do this three times and they really didn't like it. It's difficult for them to talk to their mates when they are not at eye-level any more! By being consistent about this, I've got my message across and they really seem to have improved. They have learned that if they don't shut up, they're going to have to stand for quite a long time. I've cut standing down to no more than three students now and reduced the time they stand. (Primary teacher)

This strategy is highly effective. The idea is to find a way of isolating a student from their peers, yet keeping them involved in a positive way as far as possible. The strategy is at its best if you behave towards standing students as if they were still sitting and contributing to the lesson. You can still be pleasant and let them stand there until the message sinks in. If you can, try to give plenty of positive feedback by asking questions and accepting answers from students who are standing.

Once you have established this in a consistent way, you can warn students they will have to stand if they cannot cooperate with the rest of the class ('If you can't listen when you're sitting, you'll have to listen when you stand'). This can make the strategy more effective because fewer students will be standing at any one time – preferably no more than two. The fewer students there are, the greater the isolation. Avoid at all costs creating a situation where several standing students can chat across the room, or the strategy will fail. Make sure that you never ask more than one student at a time to stand. There is no point whatsoever in saying: 'I need you six to stand up right now!'

What do you do if the class still will not stop talking? Ask yourself what rewards there are for listening. The carrot of learning (surely enough for many students?) may not be enough to reward those who need more obvious rewards for listening.

- Are there enough 'Well done!' rewards for listening?
- Do students hear their names used frequently enough in praise?
- Are there any privileges won for listening instead of chattering?

- Are there team or house points?
- Are there rewards such as a choice offered about how time can be spent?
- Do you emphasize praising an 'adult' response from children?

There are no magic wands to be waved here and you will need to be inventive about rewards for behaving well. Even so, chatterbox classes are not going to respond unless there are rewards built in. If individual students behave in a better way, and hear 'Well done Ruth, that's a really grown up way to listen', or 'Brilliant Simon, well listened and good concentration', you are rewarding what you want and being positive. Making children stand up is effective but negative and therefore needs to be counterbalanced with positive praise.

What do you do if standing up does not work?

> I got them to stand up, and that was quite effective, but it blocked the view of children behind them – and sometimes, giving them a literally higher profile isn't such a good idea. I have my class organized sitting at desks arranged in a double horseshoe, so I use the space on the floor in front of me to sit difficult kids on the carpet. It has the same strong message, and removes them from the children they are disturbing without making them so obvious. Another device I've used in PE, and also during groupwork when someone is being uncooperative, is to single out a difficult child and say 'Look, I want you to sit here and *watch* how the others work. When you think you've got the hang of it, and can move without bumping into other people . . . discuss things without quarrelling – then you can join in.' Of course they know how they are supposed to be behaving, but it removes them temporarily, like 'time out', while reinforcing the behaviour you want and pretending it's not a punishment! (Year 5 teacher)

A variation is to remove a student from a group working on a project or activity and have them watch another group working well. You may need to sit them close, but not sitting as part of the group they are watching. They need to be on the sidelines.

The worst that can happen is that you enter the classroom and it is so noisy that you are unable to hear yourself think. You cannot start without making a very loud signal, but there are other visual signals that are strong.

> I have recently taken to using the non-verbal cue of writing a message such as 'Quiet Please' on the board. This has been effective as someone has always seen me doing it, then the quiet has begun to spread throughout the class. (Trainee teacher)

If writing 'Quiet Please' does not work, you could keep writing 'I'm ready to start and need quiet before I can teach you' as many times on the board as it takes to get quiet. Keep your back to the class and continue to write. If you fill the board, rub everything clean and start writing it repeatedly. You may think that this sounds insane, but it does work because you persist until it does. Students soon tire of what they are doing and take an interest. They will 'Shhh' each other. Follow this with a genuinely meant 'Thank you'. Overuse of this or any other strategy will diminish it, so you will need other ways to get attention. However, followed up positively, it is effective.

Ask the class why Dan is noisy

Dan's demand for attention is high. He makes noises, shuffles papers and continually attempts to borrow students' equipment. This is an excuse to make contact and disrupt others. As innocently as you can, stop the lesson dead in its tracks and ask if anyone can tell you why Dan wants to misbehave. You will find that (done well) students will respond and say things like 'He wants the attention', 'He wants to be cheeky', and 'Wants to be silly so we'll all look at him.' You might even ask: 'How many of you think Dan did that just to get attention?' Once you have a list of reasons (ignore denials from Dan), your classic response is 'That's why we need to ignore him for a while, so we can all learn.'

You psychologically deprive Dan of his audience and leave him wondering who his supporters are. You can strike an agreement with the class about how many attempts to get attention would be reasonable for Dan per day, or per lesson. Asking Dan if he can think of a better way to get attention is a good starting point for breaking up his game. It does not matter if Dan cannot think of a better way. You broke up his game of let-me-see-what-I-can-do-next. No guarantees, but if you describe the noises and low-level disruption to Dan, he may phase it out of his repertoire. You will immediately need to praise him so his change of mind is recognized and validated.

Adapting your voice tone to encourage self-discipline

Teacher-talk also includes modelling politeness. You cannot say to a child that their way of speaking to others is unacceptable if you speak like that yourself. If you can say 'I don't speak to you like that' and mean it, you provide a good model. If you shout or scream at children, you are inviting them to scream back. A teacher needs to use a voice that does not sound aggressive, plaintive, bored or emotionally wrought. The tone of your speech is meant to persuade students to respond in an adult way. Enthusiasm in your voice tone is a bonus. If you sound like a nagging or angry parent, children may want to behave like the worst of petulant toddlers. Your voice needs to carry its emotional message of teacher-power (I'm in charge of the class) without being military. Sound like an adult when you say 'I'm really not happy with that', or 'Stop that now before it goes any further.' If your voice pleads like a child you will not get very far, so you need to avoid '*Pleeease* stop', sounding powerless.

Often, when pushed by a difficult class, teachers who are new to the job will resort to aggressive parental tones. According to the 1960s psychologist Eric Berne, within all of us is the admonishing parent, the adult and the petulant child, regardless of our age. Even children can sound like angry parents because they soon learn to copy the style of parental response for themselves. If you want to test your voice tone to check its adult, parent or child tone, try saying the same phrase in three different ways. The adult tone is calm and relatively emotion-free. The parent is angry and the child pleads or sounds upset:

> Adult: Tell me all about what you've been doing in the last half hour.
> Parent: What on *earth* have you been doing in the last half hour?
> Child: You've no idea how *awful* the last half hour has been for me!

Parental and childlike tones are life's unavoidable way of expressing ourselves. They cannot be eradicated, nor should they be. However, they need to be kept in check in the classroom because of the effect that they have. The aim is to maintain an adult-to-adult tone of voice as far as possible.

You may feel that your step-by-step classroom scripts have become tedious and you would prefer to encourage self-discipline. When you start teaching, scripts are necessary if your students are not particularly self-disciplined. Drop the detail once you have established clearly the five or six things that you expect. Expectations can lead to self-discipline because you are encouraging the students to think rather than follow commands from you all the time. In Chapter 2 we saw how an infant school headteacher used her magic wand for her five wishes. Adapting this, you can develop a shorthand where 'Ready to listen' means seven things that you never need to say. The class knows your seven things because you have set them up in the first place. For example, one teacher I know uses a signal to remind his class of his expectations. He taps either one or other of his shoulders as he asks for quiet. The signal is clear and visible and means:

- stop;
- put things down;
- hands off the desk;
- feet still;
- mouths closed;
- eyes on the teacher/board;
- ready to listen.

Incidentally, some teachers would prefer 'Hands on the desk'. Whatever your preference, make sure that equipment is pushed away from fidgeting hands, otherwise you will experience the creep of fingers towards a pen or a pencil. Reminders for students are coded messages such as 'We're not ready yet', meaning that a checklist of actions is not being followed. Encouraging self-discipline needs a great deal of praise and a complete absence of sarcastic comment, such as: 'Well done at last! What took you so long?' A simple 'Well done' and a swift move onwards to the content of your lesson is quite enough compared with a major nagging speech about the time that it took. What student ever remembered how long it took last time?

Without encouraging self-discipline you can have a riot on your hands the minute you turn your back. Repressive, rule-driven classrooms give students no responsibility for their own behaviour. If the only discipline is enforced control and step-by-step instructions, students can become very difficult because they do not have to think. Enforced control is far removed from a civilized personal code of conduct. A better aim is to encourage responsibility for being ready, being polite, settling down to a task, considering other students and completing work. All of these give you opportunities to praise responsible behaviour, saying 'Well done for being ready on time', or noticing things that students do such as: 'I noticed that you settled down quickly, by the way. That's good.' Always remember that children eventually want to be adults. Encouraging them to be adult and responsible takes them further down that path.

Establishing self-discipline may sometimes feel like you are chipping away with a geological hammer, reminding and praising your students. Adult phrases and questions for your script that encourage self-discipline are ones that demand a response:

> What are you going to do about it?
> How could you sort that out?
> Why are you telling *me*?
> Tell me what you think you could do to change that.
> You two, sort yourselves out and tell me when you have.
> It's your responsibility to improve that.
> Organize your work so it doesn't create a problem for anyone else.
> Think how to change that for yourself.
> Remember how we move around the room.

Your aim is to code your messages to the point where students begin to look after themselves and accept what you want of them. One-liners, single words and mimed gestures all have their place in your repertoire of management (I can think of occasions when many of the examples I have listed would be accompanied by a long pause, sometimes an uncomfortable one). Students need thinking time to respond to any of these coded messages. Remember: specific requests ('Put that pen down and listen, please') do not require much thought on the part of students. Requests to imagine, sort out, improve or change things demand much more.

Self-responsibility happens in other ways. You can give students responsibility for something and make them feel very important.

> I have a system of secret monitors for various jobs. The class has to try to guess who is the monitor and what they are doing. I just tell them there are three secret monitors today. There is often a magical tidying going on, or a student gives out books without being told to. I reward the monitors with a personal sticker if they do a good secret job. The best is probably when we go down to the assembly hall or to the playing field. I have 'walking monitors' whose job it is to set the perfect walking pace and keep to this. Because it's a secret, the other students tend to walk well anyway and try to guess who is the monitor. They miraculously follow the code of behaviour for walking sensibly. This only works if they already know there's a secret monitor. (Year 2 teacher)

This works partly because it is a guessing game, but the fact that you have handed over responsibility to monitors can put you in the background. You can leave the rest up to the students themselves.

Questions for reflection

- What coded messages can you remember from your schooldays?
- How do teachers set noise levels?
- What does 'settling time' actually mean?
- Why would 'concentration time' be worth aiming for?
- How can you adapt teacher-talk to encourage self-disciplined students?
- If you ask a question, does that mean students are obliged to answer?
- Why is it worth learning to pause?
- What would be your strategy if a class does not stop chattering?
- What aspects of noise limitation are defined by demonstration and explanation?

Checklist summary

- Continually 'Shhh-ing' a class is a waste of breath.
- Turning questions into statements of need is effective.
- All misbehaviour has some purpose and the most difficult to deal with is behaviour that is intended to disrupt lessons without obviously doing so.
- Most students benefit from knowing what to do first when they begin a task.
- Short specific phrases within your script are often coded messages.
- The more effective a coded message, the less intrusive and time-wasting it is.
- Establishing self-discipline may sometimes feel like you are chipping away with a geological hammer.

Tell them what you want, and give them a big beamy smile when they do it. If you say anything at all, keep your voice upbeat and dish out the praise.

(Primary teacher)

More about praise

I have heard teachers say: 'Well, I'd praise him if he did something to deserve it.' Other teachers will tell you, 'This lot? They need overpraising to get the best out of them.' Who is right? Teachers are professional critics of children's work, always on the lookout for ways to improve it. Part of their job is to see mistakes, correct them and decide what the next steps will be. Children are not so aware of the next steps themselves, so they need far more positive feedback than can be imagined. Over-praising is not exactly a criminal offence. It would be rare for any new teacher to be criticized for over-praising the work and efforts of their class. Over-praising can build a positive ethos that allows you to be far more effective when you need to reprimand and be negative. Praise, praise and more praise by the bucketful will always be more effective than stamping on every false move that students make. The days when teachers enforced by fear are hopefully long gone, but some teachers still want to be 'in authority', enforcing rather than being assertive. An authoritarian stance can easily push aside praise to the point where the classroom is not a rewarding place to be. The atmosphere becomes humourless, the teacher stonefaced and military. The usual excuse for this is that there are high standards of student behaviour to maintain, standards that need reinforcing.

Beginners generally know the theory of being positive and reinforcing with praise, but this needs plenty of practice. Giving generous quantities of meaningless praise instead of praise that is specific to effort and achievement does not reinforce anything. It takes time to learn for yourself what is effective and even to discover how numerous your students' praiseworthy efforts are.

Praising specific aspects of their work reinforces what you value. Experienced teachers are likely to value students' efforts by internalizing negative comments and searching for something to praise in what they see. The praise sounds genuine and not diminished by sarcasm or use of the word 'but'. Students soon pick up on the 'Very good *but* could do better' style of praise. The word 'but' cancels out the praise that went before it. Of course students could do better, but they have probably heard that a million times from their parents. Praise needs no 'ifs' and 'buts' transmitted by your tone of voice, gesture and facial expression. There is nothing wrong with striving for high standards if the route to these is positive.

Teachers are very good at giving praise but not always very good at praising themselves. If you try to write a list of positive flattering comments about yourself and a list of negative ones, the negative list is almost always longer (I have done this occasionally with a group of trainees and I know they find it far harder to flatter themselves than criticize). Negative comments are much easier to make, and the skill in a classroom is to be positive when you observe negative behaviour. Throw the switch. Even if you think it is not being true to yourself, you do it because the outcome will change how students respond.

A way to think of this as a personal teaching challenge is that behaviour is a student's responsibility; praise is your responsibility. You expect your students to behave with a sense of responsibility, so praise on its own is not all you need to think about. A number of students are very adept at anticipating your latest ruse to manage them. You can see the wheels going round in some of their brains as they try to find new ways to subvert your latest strategy. Those wonderful phrases that refer to rules (Chapter 3) are still a bit of a challenge for some children. Praise is necessary to undermine negativity, but the subtleties of it lie in descriptions of what you see.

Describing what you see and 'proximity praise'

Sometimes the fastest route to good behaviour is to 'cut to the chase'. Describe what you see and throw responsibility back to the student. This is not being negative. You might say something that starts out with a positive compliment. for example:

> Darren, you're doing lots brilliantly today and you need to think carefully about what you need to do next.
> Darren, I know you're better than this. I can see you're not behaving the way we like in this class. What are you going to do about it?
> Darren and James, I see you're in difficulty. Sort yourselves out.
> Darren, think.

Darren may click into self-responsibility mode, but in response to 'What are you going to do about it?' he may say 'Gonna do nothing!', and you will need to follow this with 'That's not an option. You may not like what we're doing, but I know you're capable and can do this.' In effect, you flatter Darren with praise by saying he's capable, and may want to add: 'Make a good start and I'll check your work in a couple of minutes.' Darren has been noticed, his behaviour registered, some attempt made to throw back responsibility and a backup plan used if Darren has said 'Nothing!' Best of all, you have managed to flatter Darren at the same time as you ticked him off. Reverting to your previous description, you could add: 'I've seen you work really well Darren, and that's so good to see.' Whatever you decide, depending on the student, describe and attempt to put the responsibility where it belongs – with the child. Following this with praise helps to focus attention on the contrast between the good and bad. You catch Darren off-guard because he does not expect praise. All this may seem low-key compared with 'Brilliant Darren. Well done!' but it is specific, positive and active, sounding far more true to life than an over-rehearsed 'Well done!' Reserve 'Well done!' for later; however, do not rule out 'Well done Darren for making such a good start!'

If you want to encourage self-discipline in students, a well-tested strategy is to use 'proximity praise'. This is quite genuinely thanking (praising) students or groups who are sitting nearest to those who are not yet functioning. Imagine you are trying to refocus the class part-way through a lesson. 'Thank you Kirsty. Thank you Peter. Thank you Sarah' can be said in warm tones as you notice students are ready. Pick the students who are in proximity to the most difficult students because this removes their audience. Gradually reduce the volume of your voice as an increasing number of students give their attention and make sure that you thank students by name. You need to be heard speaking sufficiently loudly for all to hear you, but not so loud that it has no effect on the atmosphere.

In addition, proximity praise can include descriptions of good responses. These are powerful and the examples that follow could be used either when students are waiting or when they are working at a task. When you work with older children there is sometimes a culture of group teasing if a student is praised, so the phrasing needs to be different. In the most adult of tones, cool and off-hand, you might say 'Thanks Kirsty for getting your book out' and 'Thanks John, Sarah and David for making the effort.' You are not exactly praising, but it has a similar effect. You certainly need to avoid singling out only one student and praising their saintly behaviour, as in: 'You're behaving brilliantly, Peter!' That piece of exaggeration could get Peter bullied after school and is non-specific (therefore useless). Your body language and tone of voice do not want to transmit 'He's one of my favourite students', which it could if you really think Peter is behaving brilliantly. It is far better to signal that you are organizing the whole class, eliminate any emotional favouritism in your speech and mention Peter as just one of several students. Teachers of older students need to turn some of these into a form of adult-toned polite thanks, as in 'Thanks Kirsty, I can see you've got the book we're using'. In almost matter-of-fact tones, you can describe what you see.

Describing what you see

'I can see Kirsty has her book open and is ready to read.'
'I can see that Peter arranged the space on the desk so nothing gets in anyone else's way.'
'There's still litter on the floor and two of you near the window have already picked some of it up.'
'John, Sarah and David are making a real effort. Thanks for that.'
'I can see at least five people not working.'
'I can see we're not all ready.'
'I can see you're upset . . .'
'I can hear you don't know how to ask.'
'There are so many bits of paper on the floor we can't leave the room yet.'
'I'm sure this room can look better before we leave it.' [*pause*]

Another way to describe what you see is to use 'I notice . . .' , or 'I notice, by the way . . .', both of which can help to elicit useful information. The phrases work better if you end them with a tone of voice rising in pitch to imply that they are questions. The French do this as a cultural style. They turn a statement into a question by ending it on an upward inflection. If you say to a student 'I notice you've spent a long time finding out about the Greeks?', or 'I notice you're quite excited?' and pause, they will often volunteer information. You can use this to share the student's experience with them and sound genuinely positive. Using a different tone of voice, you might say 'I noticed you put in a lot of effort', or 'I noticed you improved your writing'. The fact that you are declaring that you noticed is positive.

Describing what you see avoids judgements. The reality is that a student worked hard *this time* and put in the effort so 'I can see you've worked hard this time' is better than 'You're good at this'. It may surprise you to discover you can accuse students and still thank them. Imagine a teacher who is struggling to retain Darren's attention in order to stop his misbehaviour:

Teacher: Darren! Are you listening? [*said loudly, assertively and bordering on the confrontational*]
Student: Yeh. [*said with some reluctance*]
Teacher: Thank you. [*said genuinely, quietly and not sarcastically*]

Perhaps you will take your students by surprise by thanking them when they really expect an escalation of the impending confrontation. Your 'Thank you' gives respect back to the student, especially an older student. It also treats behaviour consistently by reinforcing what is desirable. It is tempting not to thank or praise difficult students because of the emotional wind-up they give you. The cooperative ones are much easier to praise.

Using 'by the way' as a form of praise

In order not to make too much of a meal of your thanks, you can add a 'by the way' so that you say things like 'Yes Rosie, that's right. And thanks for putting up your hand, by the way', or you could say 'And by the way, thanks for being polite.' This tells the student that their good behaviour was noticed. By contrast, it is almost an invitation to misbehave when you say to a class 'You behaved really well this lesson', or 'You really did brilliantly yesterday.' When you say 'You've really worked hard at your reading, by the way', this refers to work and effort, not behaviour as a generalization. Even difficult students can be praised specifically for efforts, as in: 'You've really shown how long you can sit working without getting out of your seat. Well done.'

Description allows students to credit themselves, does not ignore errors and is powerful because it is mostly free of value judgements. However, notice that an encouraging comment has been added, such as 'Well done!' Some teachers prefer an enthusiastic 'Well done *you*!', which has that extra personal dimension. Given with the right tone of voice it can be used with adults (the right tone of voice is an adult one anyway). If you want to try this for yourself, imagine that one of your students is actually aged about 30 and praise them in an adult way. You will be surprised how effective it can be. 'By the way' can become a good habit, showing that you still care how students in your care behave. You exchange enforcement for appreciative 'by the way' comments, encouraging gently and praising the values you want to promote.

Descriptive praise

'You concentrated so hard on that, you didn't stop for a second before you finished. Fantastic for doing that!'
'The extra time you put into this is really paying off. Well done you!'
'I notice you used a sharp pencil to get those coordinates right. That makes your graph easier to understand. You really did well.'
'I like the detail you added about the delicatessen in your story. That shows you understand the power of a good adjective. Well done!'
'You've thought about safety and used plastic goggles and gloves. I didn't need to remind you. Well done.'
'You completed seven maths problems and set them out carefully. Each one was more difficult than the last and yet you concentrated for a full hour. That means real progress. You had difficulty with numbers five and six. You got those wrong so we'll need to find out why and put that right.'

Descriptions are less likely to make a child think 'I was brilliant last time, but what will I be next time?' A value judgement such as 'Wow! That's a really good score, you're brilliant' is not so useful as 'Wow! That's a good score this time. You must have worked really hard to get that.' If you concentrate on the effort, you are much more likely to encourage tenacity and persistence. There is every reason for students to continue to make the effort because next time is still a clean sheet. Once you describe someone as clever or brilliant they have to live up to that. Which is probably why the life of a world-famous concert pianist can be so difficult. Such fame can be compromised by a less-than-brilliant performance every time, demanding rigorous practice to keep up the skill. Even a concert pianist performs less brilliantly some days than others, so there is no such thing as brilliance without a cost.

Points, stickers, stars and marbles

I have played a game with my class which lasts all day. It's a variation on raising your hand and waiting for silence. I clap my hands twice and then count on my fingers to five. If the class is quiet by then, they receive a point. If not, then I get a point. If they win at the end of the day, then they get a class point. (Trainee teacher)

All day, for just one class point? Giving only one class point after a whole day illustrates a fundamental principle of rewards. It is not so much the reward itself as the game of getting it that is so appealing. There really is no need to be over-generous, awarding class points every five minutes. There are stickers and stars to be had by the bucketful but what do you want to achieve? I have known teachers who gave individuals only a silver or gold star, although they were more generous in verbal praise and 'smiley faces' stickers. Silver and gold were greatly prized because they were rarely given. Nobody got a gold star every week, or even a silver if they did not merit it for their effort. Three silver stars meant they had a gold star. This may seem rather a mean-minded approach, but you would soon discover that too many 'high reward' stickers can create unrealistic expectations. If students expect stickers and points during every lesson, you lose the greatest of all stickers. That is the one a child gets unexpectedly. You also need to think about how those students feel who rarely get rewards, because it is not much fun watching other people being rewarded frequently. A better way to reward is to give plenty of verbal praise and a few stars and stickers that are worth having. Not everyone would agree with me here. Some teachers give stickers every 15 minutes and find that it works for them. Whatever you decide, you need a hierarchy of stickers similar to tin, bronze, silver and gold if the stickers are not specific.

Stickers and stars have a long tradition in schools, even at secondary level. If they did not work they would have been abandoned years ago. They are like a tally chart of success, although in recent years target stickers and badges have gained favour. These are rewards that also suggest a target for specific improvement. Whenever stickers are awarded, it is far better to add some verbal comment making it very clear why the reward has been given. Excellent spelling is an obvious example, where the context might have been 'You're getting this for remembering how to spell those difficult words we looked at last week', or 'I'm giving you this because you listened well today'.

Stickers for targets and achievement

Well done! Target achieved.
Well done for concentrating.
For careful listening.
What a star for helping!
Good playground behaviour.
Monster effort!
Excellent spelling!

Some stickers are devised by teachers themselves, and if they are graded according to difficulty they become 'target ladders'.

I can solve problems involving ratio.
I can write a percentage as a fraction of 100.
I can write tenths and hundredths as decimals.
I can sound out phonemes to build words.
I can blend and segment new words.
I can keep ideas going to the end of a story.
I can write a formal letter to a business manager.

Whatever system you devise, you will need a simple tally of points awarded or stars on a chart. Alternatively there is the system of putting marbles in a jar. The way this works is to have two jars, one for the teacher and one for the students. If the class works well, two marbles might be awarded from the teacher's jar to theirs. The reason for using jars is that there is a good loud clink when the marbles are dropped in the jars, a sound that seems to have importance for winners and losers. If the class works particularly badly, the teacher takes a marble away. When a certain number of marbles are in the students' jar, this means that they have earned some free choice time (sometimes called 'golden time'). Again, getting a marble seems to be more important than the number of marbles gained. One advantage of setting up marble jars is that when something goes really well in your lesson, you need do no more than enjoy putting a marble in the jar, mid-sentence if you like.

> I have begun to use the 'marbles in a jar' system of rewards, but I am unsure how this will work at this stage. I've given each table a jar, but there seems to be more focus on competition between tables than about filling the jar. Also, one child keeps stealing marbles from other tables if she doesn't think they deserve them! I intend to keep it going, but will be much meaner with the marbles to see how that works. (Primary trainee teacher)

Giving each table its own marble jar is a big mistake. Use two only, the teacher's jar and the students' jar. They need to be placed in a position where they cannot be tampered with easily. Also, they need to be used in a consistent way and never as the result of bargains or bribes.

Teachers can be very creative when they want to find rewards. For example, one teacher I know sets up groupwork so that the group can earn points for lower noise levels. Twenty points gets the group a reward, such as first choice of tune on an MP3 music player during a free choice time or a wet playtime. Another has tooth-rotting confectionery, and another has a swatch of special art papers from which the rewarded student has first pick. If tangible rewards are not to your liking, remember that being given time for free choice activities is also a great motivator. After all, time off for good behaviour is a standard reward, even in prison communities.

Improvement suggestions

Giving students some suggestions for improvement implies that there is an element of choice and responsibility involved. In the two examples that follow, Year 6 students have been doing a project designing a holiday brochure for visiting Kenya, covering aspects of literacy and geography. The comments made by the teacher are free of value judgements (excellent, very good, poor). Instead, the teacher has provided specific feedback about what works well and what does not. There follows a suggestion for improvement.

> Ayden, Nathaniel, Daniel – you have included pictures and text and details of cost, accommodation and activities. You haven't mentioned the landscape at all so your holiday could be anywhere.
> (*Improvement suggestion:* follow the challenge instructions given to you and check your work against the criteria.)
> Kirk – You have obviously done a lot of research for this project. You described two different kinds of Kenyan holiday. Presentation is good and you found suitable pictures.
> (*Improvement suggestion:* perhaps you could do more of your own writing and not copy so much from other sources.)

A development of this is to give peer responsibility to students for finding good features in each other's work and suggesting improvement. This would need practice in looking at criteria and learning to describe other students' work in a positive way. Essentially you are teaching students the social skill of descriptive praise, followed by a suggestion for improvement. Both these strands can become questions: 'What are the good features of this project?' and 'What is your suggestion for improvement?' The subplot of this is that often, students are taken by surprise when a compliment unexpectedly comes from one of their peers. Praise that has impact is often simple description that allows students to praise themselves. Presenting the description as data without value judgements can invite thoughts such as: 'I organized my group and kept to time', 'It was hard, but I did it!' or 'I can see how to improve this now.'

Teaching is one of those activities where a student's reward for success is to be given an even harder task to do. Stars and stickers draw a line across this and avoid upping the difficulty until students actually fail. Improvement suggestions need to be *suggestions* not *requirements*, otherwise you could easily demoralize your class. However, uncritical praise is not very useful in itself because there is nothing for which to strive. You might ask students: 'Do you want an improvement suggestion this time?' In theory the student has agreed to this. Improvement suggestions are an attractive option where students are doing a project or activity that still has some way to go. They are a waste of time if the project is already finished. A vague 'next time you do this kind of thing' might never be remembered. Formative praise which has suggestions attached needs implementing quickly enough to be worthwhile. Suggestions for improvement always imply that there is work still to do. An adult might welcome this, but plenty of students are more focused on task completion than they are on task improvement.

A slightly risky strategy is to ask: 'Can I make a suggestion for improving your behaviour?' The answer will most likely be a 'No' or a reluctant 'OK then', but it is worth trying this with some students. Since you have asked and did not just tell them, they may respond a little more positively. Nothing ventured, nothing gained. You could start by saying all the things that are good about the student's behaviour before making suggestions for improvement. Clearly, a great deal depends on the relationship that you have with your students because they need to feel that they are being helped, not criticized.

'First warning, John'

Many beginners forget two important questions: (1) which behaviour receives the *most* attention for this student?; and (2) why are some students in my class addicted to getting attention? The answer is that for them, behaving badly is a much quicker way of getting noticed. Children very soon learn what gets them the most attention. Analyse what you see and be determined to give more attention to good behaviour, so that students realize their bad behaviour gets them nowhere.

You hope not to need warnings and sanctions to do this, but you will when other strategies do not work. Sanctions are a last resort, so if you give them to students they need to be successful. Give warnings first and be aware that warnings and sanctions fail:

- if you are inconsistent in using them;
- if you overreact to bad behaviour;
- if you use them too frequently;
- if you do not carry out what you threaten;

- if there are poor routines or few routines;
- if you have low expectations of your students;
- if you are not good at listening to students;
- if you are more interested in behaviour than effort and achievement.

Some warnings can be wrapped up in the midst of a general round-up of stray students: 'Eyes, Rachel', 'First warning, John', 'Sitting properly please, Sarah', 'Pen down, hands on the desk, Peter.' The rule of thumb here is to abandon warnings which are so long-winded that they shift the focus of the lesson. Go for a pithy phrase and press on, engaging students' minds. Warnings are more effective if they are brief. Moving on is more important than bringing the lesson to a grinding halt, mainly because students find concentrating difficult enough without the distraction of a nagging speech.

Warnings need to be given in stages, much along the lines of football yellow card/red card infringements. In some schools, the red card means the student has to go to another teacher under a reciprocal agreement to isolate a student from immediate classmates. The most commonly used strategy for warnings is a 'three strikes and you're out' approach. For a first offence the student's name goes on the whiteboard. A second offence results in a tick against that name. Third offences invite time out or being sent to another member of staff. An important aim here is to keep the rest of the class on-side, so some teachers will do their stepped discipline dispassionately and retain a sense of humour within the rest of the class. Instead of yellow cards and names on the board, there are reward cards with smiley faces and miserable ones for offenders. If you try this, make sure that you use them at quite different times so that a reward card is not given to one student at the same time as an offender card is given to another.

Sanctions are either missed privileges or a form of community service. Loss of privilege, such as being able to have free time on a computer or losing breaktime, is well tried. In dire cases, students miss the school trip or a one-off school visit. Some students miss out on sessions involving visiting musicians or artists if they are likely to disrupt the session. Beyond these are the usual community service sanctions, such as picking up litter or tidying, cleaning and organizing (I cannot think of a useful sanction, but perhaps this is the point of them). You could ask students what sanction would fit the crime and then set that. If you are lucky, there might be a spontaneous apology, but that is more a hope than an expectation. Detentions are still used by some schools as a way of losing personal freedom. Not every teacher agrees that detentions are a good punishment, but they do work well for some schools.

Punishments need to be small

Any punishment that you devise has a limited effect because punishing does nothing much to rehabilitate a difficult student. It temporarily prevents further misbehaviour by suppressing it. You need to dish out punishments as rarely as you have to, and without emotion. Lengthy punishments are not effective because they create resentment, especially if they are given without any warning. The last thing you want to do is create a negative atmosphere over a period of time. However difficult students might be, creating a negative classroom atmosphere on a daily basis is not much of a solution to their behaviour problems – they are likely to seek revenge when you least expect it. If you do need to impose a sanction, make sure that it is imposed in exactly the same way for the same offence because students need to know there is a scale of punishments for misbehaving. Even when you impose a sanction, refer to the behaviour you want. In the midst of your internalized anger and your imposed sanction, the truth is that even the most difficult children will need a good reason to be in your class.

The confessional

It may be too intimidating for some students, but you can ask for a written answer to the following questions (assuming that the child can read and write).

- What did I do wrong?
- Why was my action not acceptable?
- What should I have been doing instead?
- What will I do in the future?
- What have I done today to help anyone else?

A slightly grey area regarding punishment is how to deal with persistently cheeky students (this was mentioned in Chapter 2, where you were urged to refer them back to their work). Some students go further and delight in misguided humour which is actually insulting. They do not always know this. You will find that this is difficult to deal with because you could be misunderstood if you object to the jokes. Outright insult is more obvious and likely to cause any teacher a great deal of stress, along with cheek disguised as friendliness. There is a useful way to respond to these two irritants, which is to find your own versions of the following:

> I think that's a fair point to be making, but you have an insolent way of saying this that I don't like.
> I think you might be right, but I don't like the cheeky way you said it to me. It's unfriendly and insulting.

In the first response scripted here you could say, for example:

> [*As warmly as possible*] I think that's a fair point.
> [*As coldly as possible*] But you have an insolent way of saying this that I don't like.

If this has no effect, you will need to resort to small punishments for persistent insolence (there is always the classic 'I wouldn't speak to you like that'). Every situation is slightly different, so I am sticking my neck out by recommending an actual script to use. Before you punish, register the fact with the student that you find the cheek is offensive to you. Left unchecked, you are sending a clear signal that you do not object to cheeky students when actually you do. You may like the student but you do not like their behaviour. Usually, cheeky students will push and push to see how much they can get away with; often they are very confident speaking to teachers. Stopping their cheeky response may cause you to say: 'I'm sure you want to be friendly, but it is unfortunately sounding like being cheeky. I don't want to think about warnings and punishments, so let's see if you can change the way you speak to me.' The threat is in the background, you have stated how you felt about being spoken to in that way and you have showed that you are prepared to follow it through. You are looking for the opposite of cheek which is politeness, so that needs to be a target for the insolent student. Avoid any sarcasm, however, as it is the very ingredient of cheeky behaviour that will be mirrored back.

More about offering choices; blank refusal

Students are fooled into thinking that they have made the choice themselves when the choices are actually very limited. There is really no choice about attending school and everything flows from there. The illusory choice is to cooperate or live with the consequences. When you offer a choice and say what the consequences are, you present this to students as if they themselves are in control of their destiny. Notice how consequences are clearly spelled out here.

> Peter, if you continue to annoy, you will get a second warning. If that doesn't have any effect you'll have to stay back and explain yourself. You may be excluded from the class. Mary and Bethany, you have a choice: either work together and use quieter voices, or one of you will sit somewhere else. Is that clear?

If Peter, Mary or Bethany still fail to work well, you have every right to say 'Peter, I gave a choice and you ignored that. Take your books and work over there please. I'll have a look soon to see what you've done.' Choices defuse confrontation. In the face of a stubborn refusal to do something, you can only present choices and the consequences for not making a good decision. If you have given no warning, you have no reference point for your next action.

Perhaps your greatest fear is of blank refusal to give attention or to stop disrupting. Imagine that a power struggle develops when you ask Peter to move to a seat nearer to you. A confrontation is imminent as he refuses for the second time to move. At this point you may need an escape route because Peter is enjoying the confrontation. A solution is to keep calm, give him a third chance and back this up with a consequent threat of loss of time. At the third refusal, all you can do is put life on a backburner because there is no way you will win in such a confrontation. You can say, for example, 'You've chosen to refuse and you've chosen to ignore me, so we'll need to look at that later. Sit there and do nothing or choose to work and let me know if you need help.' You then try to keep the rest of the class on your side, turning away physically from Peter (turn your back on him). Say something like 'We may need to ignore Peter's behaviour until it changes.' In the final analysis, with extremely difficult students, you may be thrown back to another teacher's help and the behaviour policies of the school. There is no shame whatsoever in seeking help from more experienced teachers.

Point blank refusal is always a choice between 'do it now, or live with the consequences'. If Peter refuses to go to another seat and shouts 'You can't make me!' he is quite right, but he is also choosing to take things further. Agree with him and say 'No, I can't *make* you, but there will be consequences you won't like.' Expect mutterings and probably the slamming of a book down on a desk if he changes his mind and complies. Just ignore the frustrated behaviour so long as he finally settles down to work. You can hardly expect Peter to move with good grace and this is no time to complain about the *way* he settles. Just be thankful that he is moving.

> I have had to use a particular strategy with stubborn students so that neither party loses face. For example, I asked one child to move because she was being disruptive at reg-istration. She stubbornly sat, not moving. I did not want to lose face with the class so I told the child she could take the register to the office (a privilege) but that she would have to sit where I had asked when she came back (win/win!). This worked! (Trainee teacher)

This probably worked because the culprit was removed from the classroom and had a few moments to contemplate their behaviour, time to calm down and think. Choices are warnings in themselves. 'If you want to stay with the rest of the class, then behave like the rest of the class' is a strongly-worded warning, phrased as a choice. Sometimes you may have to spell out the either/or choice to students, as in: 'You now have two choices. Either you do this now . . . or you . . . Make up your mind and let me know.' Most students will opt for the easy way out, so all you need to do is persist and let them think that they have made the choice themselves. Truly smart students may say that they do not want either of the choices you have offered them, but that has to be met with 'Not an option'. Sometimes the way that you rephrase a familiar warning helps to boost its impact, as in: 'If you can't *behave* like the rest of the class, you can't *be* with the rest of the class.' If the student still refuses, you are in a no-win battle and must revert to the advice given in Chapter 4 ('You're choosing not to do this, but you'll have to stay behind and there *will* be con-sequences. I'm not going to discuss it any longer'). The line of least resistance for the student will be to comply eventually. This is unlikely to happen imme-diately. Remember: you are not running a military camp, barking orders at soldiers. It is a classroom, so give difficult students time to decide that it is easier to comply.

Consequences after warnings

- The certainty of consequences must be reinforced with small punishments for warnings to mean anything.
- A consequence not followed up is a consequence undermined.
- Provided that punishments are small ones, they will not be resented.
- Allow time to pass, then find something positive to say.

Punishments that span more than one lesson are not very useful. Avoid greeting a difficult student you punished yesterday by saying 'Sit over here by yourself, so I can keep an eye on you'. The message you will give is that you have no intention of wiping the slate clean and treating the student fairly. By all means remind the student that you need help and cooperation today, but avoid an ongoing punishment with all the extended negativity that this will create. The most difficult of students still need to relate to you in a positive way if they are to begin cooperating.

Time out

Time out is an extreme form of ignoring in which a student is sent to another part of the room, another classroom or is parked outside the classroom. Some schools use the medical room if it is free. Of course, time out is only effective if students do not want to be isolated. Some are quite keen to do nothing, so there need to be threats of further sanctions when imposing this. Through time out, the student who craves attention is denied it. You need to make a clear statement to the offender, such as 'I put you outside because you were not doing as I asked you' (or another reason). Rather like dealing with a very young child, the search is then on for opportunities to give back some praise the second you can on the student's return. A rule of thumb is that you impose a time out of one minute for every year of the student's life, followed by a 'Thank you for calming down.' If this seems a problem for older students, I can assure you that 'Thank you for calming down' can be said in adult tones of cool off-hand, face-saving speech. The temptation on a student's return is to make a meal of your thanks. The bad blood between teacher and offender will persist if you hang on to the crime that you have punished as if it is a means of exerting power. For example, you would not say 'You see? You can behave when you want to!', because quite clearly the student did not behave willingly. Returners to the classroom are generally compliant because they did not like the time out, not because they are motivated to behave well (see Chapter 8 concerning the 'disappointment' routine when returning from time out).

Students who dislike being isolated generally have a strong desire to get back into the group. I have seen this happen many times, particularly if a student is isolated by being made to sit at a desk facing the wall. Imagine that Callum has been warned already about clowning around. He has had his final warning and has been moved well away from other students, who are still sitting on the carpeted area of the classroom. For a time Callum sulks and wants nothing to do with his peers. Soon he makes subversive attempts to join in with the rest of the group, putting his hand up even though now technically he is not part of the action. This signals an opportunity to win him over. You can make your first contact and say something to the effect: 'I'll see how you are in three minutes and maybe you'll be able to join us Callum, but I'll need to be sure you're ready' (do this with the minimum of eye contact and fuss). You need to be consistent about the sequence of time out events. Callum's re-entry to the group is almost as important as the warnings that got him isolated.

Isolation strategy

- Warn Callum.
- Give him a second warning, offering choices – work well or be isolated.
- Isolate Callum, giving him a time limit to cool off.
- Watch for any signals that Callum wants to be part of the group again.
- Warn Callum that his re-entry is imminent.
- Invite him back, thanking him for calming down and cooperating.

When you use this strategy, be sure that you know how long Callum has been in a time out. Younger students may need an electronic timer so that their six minutes' time out is signalled. A timer can help you also to remember when Callum's time is up. The timer signal has to mean 'When you hear the timer ring I'll be asking if you're ready to come back. You don't need to move. Wait to be asked.' A teacher's preference is important here, so you may wish to have a time out area in the classroom and an automatic return once the timer rings. That way, if you are consistent, nothing is ever said. The student simply returns after cooling off. Note the recommendation here, 'Wait to be asked', not 'Wait to be told'. The difference is subtle and may amount to the same thing, but sends out a better message.

When I first began teaching an experienced teacher said to me: 'Never start anything you can't finish.' He meant that if I wanted to use time out and shouted 'Get out of this class!', I would need to be pretty sure the student would go. Chances are that if I shouted, the student would shout back or even swear at me creating a no-win fight. In my first school post, I saw a young colleague dragging a Year 6 boy to the headteacher's office. Part-way, the boy won the competition and ran off home. This colleague's attempt to drag a student who refused was no more impressive than dragging a screaming toddler out of a supermarket.

There are obvious problems with sending students out of the room. Where do they go and what do they do? If there is a window in the door, they may try to make faces at the rest of the class, which is the last thing you want. If they are regular offenders, they may hide. In some large schools, students easily lose themselves with an excuse that they are taking a message to another classroom. Specify where students are supposed to stay for time out and for how long. Older students may need to hear 'until I'm ready to let you return'. During the time out period, some teachers give the student a checklist sheet which asks the student to fill in the details of why they offended and what they intend to do to remedy it. Questions such as 'What did I do that is unacceptable?' and 'What do I intend to do to fix this?' are not really meant to elicit an essay. This is just a useful occupying device and even if students screw up the paper, they are left with the problem of explaining their actions. Other teachers put a notice by a child, saying: 'Please do not talk to me. I have decided to be here and need time to cool off.'

Time out is by nature repressive and can become overused. The last thing you want to encourage is resentment, especially from girls. You may think this a sweeping generalization, but I can assure you that if you fall out with a boy it is over much more quickly than a falling out with a girl. Resentment from girls can sometimes last for weeks, and if you do not believe this, ask an experienced teacher.

Ending on a more positive note

Turning an awkward moment into a positive one takes skill. You want difficult students to feel uncomfortable and certainly do not want to reward their bad behaviour. They feel uncomfortable when there are questions that they cannot answer. Perhaps you have asked 'Why are you persistently rude?', which is not an easily-answered question, so there may be an awkward, uncomfortable pause. So far so good, but you also used the word 'persistently' and some students do not know what that word means. You could ask them 'Do you understand that word, *persistently*?' and see what response you get. You could ask other awkwardly sounding questions to fog the situation. You will probably get the usual crop of 'Dunno. What?' and silence. The idea is to make the experience more uncomfortable, which it definitely should be by contrast with the way that the rest of the class feel. At this point you can roll out distant descriptions of how well the rest of class is working. If the class actually hears this description, the chances are that they will go into overdrive to demonstrate how well they are behaving. This may not always happen, but you say it nonetheless to keep the class on side. You sharpen the contrast of the rudeness by complimenting the way that the class is behaving so that the isolation from classmates is even greater for the rude and offending student. End by saying: 'I want to see you working well because you can, interested because that makes the time go better and involved because you're in a good class and they all want to work hard too.'

Using humour to keep the class on side

'I know you all love me and think I'm brilliant, but I need you focused and paying attention like it's the best time you listened *ever*!'
'Ben, you need to be more involved to stop yourself getting tired.'
'I want to hear the concentration going on inside your head Mark, so we all need to be quiet enough to listen to that. Well done.'
'I can hear a constant buzz from your corner. But you need to work as hard as a honey-bee so I'm sure the buzz is a good one. I don't see that yet.'
'You can do this really well, so I need to see you working so hard you're sweating a bucketful.'

Energetic determination can win through if its message is 'I'm open to being a bit of a laugh, but watch out because you still have to do what I want.' Many lessons can finish with a point-scoring plenary quiz, which can provide another opening for humour. The power of humour runs deep in a classroom where there is a good rapport with students. Imagine that you have a chance to observe Jenny, an experienced teacher with energy and imagination. In her spare time, she cooks exotic vegetarian meals and has run demonstration courses in cookery. A softy? She had a really deprived class of students from a difficult inner-city area. Jenny makes outrageous comments to her students, such as:

I'm a teacher. So you're not here to *like* me. You pupil, me nasty teacher OK? Geddit? You're here to work and even hate me if you want to. You're 'orrible and you're not working hard enough and I'm sick of you!

Jenny's body language says quite the opposite of course. The result of this frequent admonition style is that the students adore Jenny and bring her assorted gifts at morning registration. Everything she says goes against this. But the students know that whenever their teacher says they are horrible she has that glint in her eye that says 'You might be behaving horribly, but I love you to bits.' The loyalty she inspires is legendary. Jenny has gone on to become a headteacher and troubleshoot a failing school. I would guess that she understands human nature and can tap into children's minds.

Some observers would say that Jenny ran an over-strict regime and said appalling things to her students. She was not politically correct. But somehow her difficult children knew that she was concerned that they achieve something. She was involved, but recognized that to succeed she needed to bust the game that many students play, which is to go for the maximum they can get away with – she was ahead of busting the game but never short of praise for students who worked hard. She knew that there were times when she needed to be cruel to be kind.

However, humour can have unexpected results, as Joe, a trainee teacher, recounts:

> I was teaching Year 1 and I've this really fidgety kid who won't keep still. I told him I was going to pretend to hypnotize him and called him in front of me. 'Look at my eyes', I said, 'and I'll pretend to hypnotize you!' After a few seconds staring, he punched me in the eyes. It turned out he misheard the word 'hypnotize' and thought I had said 'Hit my eyes'. So he did, didn't he?

Blocking negativity in the classroom

Students will protest about almost anything. Some of them can complain, whinge and manipulate with the very best. In some cases, parents have colluded with this behaviour. They have become hooked into arguments with their children and have rarely said: 'When you've stopped having a tantrum, and stopped moaning, we can listen to you.' Some of them have never demonstrated that they mean what they say. Arguments have developed into shouting matches, achieving very little. The outcome is that unwittingly, some parents have reinforced the behaviour of students who moan and manipulate to get what they want. There are several useful comments that a teacher can use to block attempts to continue this pattern in the classroom.

1 I can hear you and I know you're upset, but we don't speak like that here because it doesn't help.
2 I'd like to hear a better way of asking for what you want, please.
3 I wouldn't talk to you like that. Try again and see if I can listen to you.
4 Try again to see if I can listen to you.
5 You've nearly got asking right. Have another go, please.

Example 1 is a teacher's attempt to change the way that a student speaks. The aim is to persuade the student to model a more adult mode of speech. Example 2 goes a step further and is a shorthand for example 1. Example 3 combines both previous examples into a two-sentence strategy. Example 4 assumes that the student already knows what to do. Example 5 tells the student that they are almost there and partly gives a compliment, partly a request. There are variants of these blocking phrases, such as 'I need to hear you . . .' and 'I don't speak like that because it doesn't help me to be heard'.

Blocking negativity also includes a 'no put-downs' policy. This means that students never put down their classmates with negative remarks, neither do they put themselves down. If you hear a student say 'I'm no good at this' or 'You're no good at this', say to them: 'That's a put-down.' You need say no more than 'That's a put-down', even if they have not the slightest clue what you are talking about – you gradually establish what a put-down is over a period of time by demonstrating that you disallow it. Students get the message eventually because they learn that you want an alternative answer or comment that is more positive. The meaning of 'put-down' is defined by example and demonstration.

Questions for reflection

- What aspects of class management derive meaning through demonstration and explanation?
- How can you be rewarding without creating high expectations about receiving rewards?
- What is a high-value sticker and a higher one still?
- What is the difference between personal rewards and whole class rewards?
- What exactly is a put-down?
- What is your immediate response to 'I'm no good at this'?
- What is on your list of small punishments that are not likely to be resented?
- How can you turn around an unrewarding classroom atmosphere?

Checklist summary

- Describe what you see and throw responsibility back to the student.
- If you want to encourage self-discipline in students, a well-tested strategy is to use 'proximity praise'.
- Rewards need to mean something or they will fail.
- In order not to make too much of a meal of your thanks, add a 'by the way'.
- Sometimes the way that you phrase a familiar warning helps to boost its impact, as in: 'If you can't *behave* like the rest of the class, you can't *be* with the rest of the class' (this is no longer a choice).
- The rule is: give a choice, then turn away and get on with something else.
- To be effective, time out has to be made clear, as in: 'I put you outside because you were not doing as I asked you.'
- Specify where students *stay* for time out and for how long.
- Time out is by nature repressive and can be overused.
- Cheeky students: first, agree that they have made a fair point, then describe how disagreeable was the way it was said.
- Gradually establish what a put-down is over a period of time by disallowing it.

7

Classroom skills

The skill of swerving

Emily's lesson

Emily does almost everything she should do according to the book. It is a hot afternoon in June and there has been a thunderstorm at lunchtime. The students are in a high state of excitement, buzzing like a box of flies. They are too hot and fidget a great deal. It is not going to be an afternoon where lining up outside the classroom to come back in again has calmed anyone down. Emily needs to swerve, but does not yet realize this and is determined to continue. She is enthusiastic, finally gets the children's attention and asks relevant questions. She gives plenty of praise and forges ahead with her plan for an interactive lesson. Why then is there still so much under-chatter and fidgeting? Why have one or two students stuck to their show-off agenda and need to be soundly ticked off every couple of minutes? Why have usually cooperative students decided to be restless and difficult? Why are one or two chewing rulers now, and others exploring their pencil cases?

Emily threatens sanctions, yet the under-chatter and silliness continues. She cannot understand quite why this is happening, because she had an excellent morning with the same class. Instead of swerving by changing her behaviour and adapting tasks, Emily decides to teach even more enthusiastically and intensely. She raises her voice and sounds over-hasty. Nothing she does is geared to calm her class and everything is designed to do exactly the opposite. Emily is more used to waking students up than calming them down. She has been taught to use her voice to reach the back row of the theatre, and her enthusiasm when doing this is usually infectious. Unfortunately Emily's solution was to sustain her loud dramatic voice whatever the situation demanded, hoping she would win through with sheer enthusiasm. Worse, as the students became difficult, her only strategy was to become even louder and more energetic. Emily began to panic.

All Emily had done wrong was to turn the volume control in the wrong direction. Her students were simply mirroring her loud enthusiastic behaviour. She

(Continued)

needed to drop the volume of her voice immediately after gaining attention to *make* them listen. This needed courage and persistence on this hottest of afternoons, consistently to lower the voice, pause and wait. It would take longer than usual to create a working atmosphere, but necessary if any work was going to be done. Loud enthusiasm was the last thing her students needed. Emily needed to learn how to calm her students by becoming calm herself.

A pitfall of classroom management is that you might forget to allow for the occasional necessary swerve when the situation demands it. Any lesson or activity taught strictly to plan, regardless of weather, responses and the students' behaviour, can fail. There is some truth in the stagecraft adage 'Never work with animals or children'. Both are unpredictable. The initial phase of a lesson stands a good chance of going to plan, but can be a heaven-sent opportunity for a difficult student to show off. The golden rule here is 'stick to the agenda', even if you need to swerve occasionally to make good use of what students offer. Focus yourself and keep students involved so that anything not relevant is sidelined. A very tough 'That's Not What We're Talking About/Try Again' policy will be needed for students who want to shift the agenda too far. You can safely assume that show-offs suffer from the temptation to shift the topic and 'torpedo' your lesson. This is not always malicious. For some students this is more a matter of finding other ways to get through their day and still feel important. One or two (usually boys) operate like cockerels in a farmyard, crowing now and again just to let you know they are there.

The easiest way to settle students might be to say 'Nobody continues until you are calm, settled, not moving and ready. Feel the calm and glue yourself to your seats.' There is some truth in the adage 'noisy teacher, noisy class'. Remember, there are moments when you need to demonstrate quiet calm. Some teachers calm students using a five-minute yoga meditation. Others immediately set a prepared written task and follow this up with quiet discussion or silent reading.

A primary teacher uses warm concrete

Next time my Year 6 class comes in 'hyper' from the football field, having fought, rowed and sworn at each other, I won't laser them. Instead, I'll give them my 'warm concrete' routine, and calm them down. They absolutely love this! What I ask them to do is sit in their seats, align their bodies – which means feet on the

(Continued)

floor, spine straight, hands resting on your knees. So, they need to close their eyes, and first they need to focus on their breathing, so they feel their breath come in. They're conscious of it in their nose, they follow it down and feel their lungs inflate, though it feels like their stomach. They feel the breath going in and out of their body. Then they have to imagine the room fills with really warm cement. They feel their feet inside their shoes (directing their minds to their feet). As the concrete fills their feet, the feet are still. They are quite happy about this. You have to reiterate 'The warm concrete is comfortable and good, and it's fixing your body so it can't move. Gradually the warm cement rises to your neck and comes over your face but never touches your face.' Time what you say slowly. 'Once you're there and can't move, you picture a place where you're alone, warm and relaxed. It might be a log fire in winter or a beach in summer. Or you might be under a tree in the sunshine, but you're in the shade.' Keep them there for a minute or two, then say: 'When I count you down from five to one, the concrete falls away and we're all ready to work.'

The skill of sustaining concentration during tasks

New teachers report difficulty in sustaining students' concentration during individual and group tasks. The beginning of a lesson may be a series of swerves because interesting feedback from students demands this. But what happens when students are supposed to be working at a set task or engaging with a series of activities?

> I'm OK at getting attention and setting tasks, but keeping kids on task after that is something else! Somehow they get too noisy and things start to happen. Somebody shoves someone else or grabs pencils. Or they just giggle instead of working properly. They chatter and spin out the task to fill the available space instead of concentrating. It's not desperate, just really annoying because it's like that every day. (Primary trainee teacher)

> I have more problems when I'm introducing my lesson than when they're doing a task. That's because there's more impact with their mates if they disrupt when they should be listening. They don't mess about so much when they are doing an individual task. Mind you, I spend some time checking that they understand the task before they do it. I ask a number of them the details of the task to see if they really understand. Then I tell them they've 15 minutes, and I wander round the room checking. If they are not getting down to work, I tell them to get on with it. I also make sure that they are doing an interesting task, if I can think of one. (Trainee teacher)

Far too many teachers assume that they are there simply to respond to problems during the on-task phase of a lesson. If you set an interesting task, many students can cope far more easily than you might imagine. You can leave them alone. By contrast, a number of them quite enjoy the additional attention and help that they get from their teacher. Some children fish for further explanation to reduce the risk of being wrong, and when they seek further help sometimes they actually reduce the quality of the task itself. They avoid having to think.

Others see doing a task as a way of bonding with their friends, an attitude which is reasonable given the need to be part of a social group. Some less able children often find ways to do the minimum and claim that they are working hard, and some bright children become bored because they are not stretched.

How can task behaviour be set up more effectively? The trainee teacher, who casually remarked that she told students to get on with it, actually did three important things. She verified understanding (thoroughly), set a deadline and checked to see if students were working. If you miss out any of these three elements of on-task behaviour, you make life more difficult for yourself. If you verify understanding more thoroughly, the implication is that the task does not necessarily need further explanation. When you do this, avoid relying on volunteers, as this invites the most able 11 students in the class to speak for the others. The chances are that you also need to ask students who you suspect do not listen. Over time, this is beneficial because it prevents students from relying on the most able to do their verifying for them. If you set a deadline you have good grounds for complaining if students do not work, and if you check on-task behaviour you reinforce codes of conduct.

Beginners are sometimes too brusque during the first minute of task 'settling time', expecting an immediately quiet working atmosphere. Some activities definitely need a couple of rowdy minutes to begin. Certain activities are very noisy by nature. Practical science, collage and design technology, for example, are activities where working noise is actually desirable. If you have engineered the transition to the task with a classic and truly effective 'when . . . then' (as described in Chapter 3), monitoring the next few minutes will be much easier. The task will be clear, the students will understand what to do first, and what to do next.

Some schools have clearly understood whole-school procedures and codes for on-task behaviour. Others rely on each class teacher to create their own code. You are trying to achieve a good working atmosphere, so it makes sense to encourage good work habits from the beginning of your on-task phase. The most common mistake witnessed in a beginner is forgetting to spell out clearly how the task is to be conducted.

Setting a task

- Make it clear what you are looking for particularly, even if this is only how clearly the work is set out.
- Talk about concentration and the importance of individual work. Make concentration a target in itself.
- Talk about 'when . . . then' as in: 'When you start this, we expect . . .', summarizing the first steps.
- Stress the need for whisper-level voices during settling time (adapt this phrase for older students).
- Set a deadline and raise expectations regarding quality and completion.

If you need to stop students to reinforce and persist, then do so. A shorthand reminder for these five ingredients is 'Remember what we expect during the task'. You can add any specific targets that the task requires; if task targets are established it becomes much easier to give praise (see Chapter 6). If you set a quality target for using descriptive words or using the correct terms in science it is so much easier to say: 'Well done. I can see you've used the correct vocabulary!' If you never have specific quality targets, then praising and encouraging is actually much harder. Once you have targets, you can follow them up with a combination of occasional praise and rapid monitoring of any off-task behaviour. The quality target gives you a chance to comment on what is missing as well as what is there, as in: 'I can't quite see you using the correct word here', or 'I can see you're trying to do this, but you need to think about . . .'

There is a hint here of the teacher showing positive interest and concern for the students' development during tasks. It is hard to spell out exactly how you would transmit this, but it can certainly make a difference if students feel that you have their development at heart. Promoting good behaviour is a great deal easier if it is sold to students as personal development and achievement. Self-discipline has been mentioned previously as a goal in behaviour management. Where students have some autonomy, can make choices and feel valued, there is a good chance that they will want to work well. I can remember years ago that I tried a strategy of calling across the classroom from time-to-time, saying, 'Are you OK, David?', 'Are you OK, Lucy?' This was my way of keeping in touch with students at a distance during tasks and it certainly worked for me. Occasionally I would vary this and ask how things were going. There are many students who think that they might just as well be on the moon as far as their teacher is concerned. Time to discuss work with individuals is always limited, so the occasional caring check helps to keep them working.

Tasks have their natural duration and it is quite a skill to anticipate when students are running out of energy. You may find that one of your tasks simply runs out of steam and you need to swerve quickly and abandon it. There will be plenty of signals if you are observant, such as fidgeting, talking with other students, fiddling with equipment and so on. When tasks die, there is nothing wrong with returning to more instructional work at the board. Younger children might be brought back to a carpeted area to review the progress made so far and set further questions to verify understanding. This would be followed by a reminder about the importance of the task and your children might go back to do more work. If time was running out, you could swerve by verifying students' understanding in a quiz. Some of the best teaching can be as a result of plans abandoned, swerves and returns to the original content of the lesson. Some of the poorest teaching can be where a trainee sticks to their plan and is oblivious of tensions, boredom, restlessness, pen-maintenance and under-chatter.

Tasks often run out of steam because they are interrupted. Messages are brought to the classroom, students are taken out, or they interrupt one another. The success of task behaviour depends on creating a culture where it becomes a very serious matter to interrupt other students. The mistake that beginners often make is to think this is trivial. They get into difficulty because their students find interruptions rather entertaining. The student who can make them laugh gains some respect from others in the class (I like him. He's a laugh!), but the disruption this causes to concentration is criminal. In some classes it is an uphill struggle to create a culture where work is valued and hindrance alienates a student from their peers. Your antidote is to say: 'You have a responsibility to other students who need to work, Peter', or 'We all have a responsibility to let others work without interruptions. Get on without interrupting anyone else please.'

The best time to do something else is just before the students run out of energy. Beginners will find it difficult to swerve when they think everything is going well, but a benchmark of experience is being able to 'read' a class so well that you change direction before the activity dies a natural death. Some of the most lively teaching I have seen involved what appeared to be time-fillers at the end of a session. Some tasks are open-ended, so that there is no question of finishing them. Examples would be creating limericks, counting, embellishing artwork, changing the plot of a story or finding information from the internet. The success of concentration during these tasks depends on having plenty to think about, not just plenty to do.

The skill of rapid intervention and more about 'Yes *but*'

> She just realized that she was reacting to what children did rather than getting in there before it happened. (Primary teacher)

A confusion in a new teacher's mind is that they are advised to react quickly, yet wait for full attention and eye-contact. They are told to exercise patience yet take quick action, remain positive but clamp down on bad behaviour. If persisting is the first rule of good behaviour management, then rapid intervention is the next. Some beginners are good at persisting to gain full attention but fail to intervene rapidly at the first sign of under-chatter, inappropriate giggling, cheers, silly noises or moans. This is understandable because they want to keep the lesson going. Unfortunately, this is a misunderstanding of what is meant by rapid reaction. A simple example of rapid reaction is to stop students in their tracks yet restart the explanation in a couple of seconds to keep the flow. This is rapid reaction but low-level response. The script in Chapter 3 demonstrates this if you re-read it as low-level interruption to the flow of the lesson. I have observed hundreds of lessons where I can count the seconds before a trainee takes necessary action. Meanwhile, noise has risen and quadrupled when all that was necessary was earlier intervention and a refocus of attention.

One example that sticks in the mind occurred in a science session looking at forces and how air acts as a force. The children were aged six or seven and gathered as a group to watch a demonstration. To prove a point about air, the trainee teacher blew bubbles and, naturally enough, the students competed to burst these. There are times when this is exactly what you would want children to do, but this was not one of them. Ideally, the trainee could have anticipated the students' reaction by saying 'When I blow these bubbles . . . I want you to watch carefully to see if they . . . ' but instead she just blew them. She could have allowed herself a surprised laugh but needed to clamp down immediately because the class was seizing on the opportunity to disrupt, giggle and be silly. Three seconds into the uproar would have been the moment, but she let it go for 10 seconds, hoping it would die away when she persisted with patience. Had she intervened at the first nanosecond of silliness, she would have clamped down on further disruption. She did not, so all she could do was wait patiently for the rabble of a class to settle down.

Sooner or later you will misjudge an instruction that you give your class. As previously mentioned, students are good at making a dive for shared equipment. In rapid intervention, you have about one second to spot that they are about to rush and another second to stop it in its tracks. The intervention has to be followed by at least three sentences of what you want (and do not want), or a reference to self-disciplined codes of conduct for sharing. Experienced teachers are most likely to have developed the habit of being on the lookout for how their students react. Beginners need to take lightning action before equipment is damaged, water spilled or a fight breaks out.

The skill of rapid intervention can be exercised to signal nothing more than a pause or a patient wait. This is where further confusion can set in for beginners. Reacting rapidly can be followed by anything you like, including waiting for attention, so long as the actual intervention is swift. React quickly, but speak slowly or you will sound agitated. If you have learned the essential skill of scanning the room every 30 seconds, you will be able to react rapidly when you need to respond. Anticipate problems by listening to the sounds that your students make, but make sure that your response is not manic and over-enforcing. It is one thing to react rapidly, but another to take appropriate action. If you hear a sound that you do not want, react quickly, but decide whether or not to take action to prevent further escalation.

Swift intervention is a great deal more draining for teachers than achieving good self-discipline from the start. A useful check on self-discipline is to see how long you can write on a whiteboard without needing to scan your class for possible disrupters. At first, you will need to talk as you write to keep students involved, turn round and check they are still with you. Later you will be able to say 'Watch closely as I write', and they will. Aim to have such well-understood codes of behaviour that you can relax and enjoy your teaching. Constantly having to react rapidly is necessary, but applied to excess it is like expecting the next bomb to go off. There is nothing more stressful for a teacher than a whole lesson of manic vigilance, looking for trouble and having to deal with it. Instead, use those self-discipline phrases mentioned in Chapter 4, striving for a working atmosphere where you do not need to keep students in check.

Sometimes good intentions to invite the adult within the child can be thwarted by students who want to hook you into a child–parent argument. They play a game called 'Yes *but*' and argue that every positive suggestion you give them has a snag:

Teacher: You could mix colours more carefully and take care with the work.
Student: Yes *but* this brush won't work properly.
Teacher: You could rinse it.
Student: Yes, *but* it wouldn't make any difference because I can't draw.
Teacher: Everybody has to start somewhere and it's getting better all the time.
Student: Yes, *but* I'm never going to be good at it, so why bother?

The child or person who plays 'Yes *but*' *always wins*. Never argue with a child over the age of two-and-a-half. Your task as a teacher is to avoid games and throw back responsibility to your students. Any way to break this cycle is better than an argument, and you can end it by making it obvious that it is a game.

You keep saying '*but*' don't you and that's not helping. Nobody ever got very far saying '*but*' and using excuses for not trying. I need you to stop saying '*but*' and work hard instead. I'll come and see how far you've got in a minute or two.

Turn away and deal with something else, allowing time for the student to realize that the game is over and work needed to be done. There is no guarantee this will work, but at least it is better than the stalemate of suggestions countered by *but*s.

The skill of being a 'snake charmer'

Teachers play many roles in their career. The aim here is to give you a picture of some alternative roles that you might find yourself playing when you progress in your ability to manage a class. In the model examples that follow, you are trying to achieve 'tennis player' or 'snake charmer', rather than 'waiter', 'plate spinner', 'lion tamer' or 'quality control officer'.

Waiters

When you first begin teaching, you are trying to understand the subtleties of all those demands and comments which students make. Consequently, you respond to what they *want* rather than what is best for them. Initially, the students may determine many of your actions because it is difficult for you to take the initiative and drive the pace of work forward yourself. You engage in the role of 'waiter', moving from group to group of students or from student to student, responding to what you perceive as their needs. Basically, you are trying to serve all the tables in the restaurant at the same time, looking to see who has finished their last course and who needs to be set another task. This is a very exhausting style of teaching because you are not exactly in control of your life. You need to move to a style to which the students respond and where *you* are dictating the pace more frequently.

Plate spinners

Once you become someone who feels that your role is to respond as fast as you can to students, you can find yourself turning into a frantic plate spinner. In this model, you try to keep everything going by literally dashing from child to child giving them an extra spin, as if they were plates on bamboo canes. This can happen if you are trying to rescue children's collapsing clay pots or limp *papier mâché*. The materials cause the inevitable panic. More usually, it means that you have transmitted to students the tacit message: 'Nothing we do here lasts for more than two minutes.' If you are dashing round keeping plates spinning, then your students are not themselves engaged in sustained pieces of work. They are dependent on you. The same plates seem to fall off the bamboo canes. All the students are likely to do, if they find you so available, is to demand even more. Watch an experienced teacher and you will see that they make clear decisions about who to talk to next, who to send away and who to keep waiting.

Lion tamer

Thankfully, this model is on the decline. In this mode you are very defensive indeed. Psychologically you keep such a distance between yourself and the students that they rarely break through the defence. Lion tamers can be heard cracking the whip and shouting 'Right, right then!', stalking round the room while students push pens on paper. More subtle versions of this are to make your style of teaching so mistrustful that you have to put a desk between yourself and the students most of the time. Even if there is no desk, children will be heard to say: 'Well, school's all right but you have to do everything their way and we can't choose anything.' The style is so rigid that the lion tamer simply dare not for a moment give any responsibility to children.

Quality control officer

A variation on this is the fault of using a desk for quality control, where all you ever see are the end-products of students' efforts rather than the thinking which has produced them or the materials which they have on their desks. If you want to help students learn, note that it is often too late by the time that they arrive at a teacher's desk. You will learn more about students' progress if you abandon the teacher's desk entirely.

Tennis player

Here you move around the tennis court (classroom) and are capable of asking questions of students who are on the baseline (the area farthest from you) as well as at the net. You can use the occasional drop shot, half-volley and move to dominate the centre of the room. You can take risks and generate a good working pace by being in a number of different areas of the classroom. If you do not believe this can be powerful, try standing at the side of the room and making students come to you rather than going over to them. Bat your questions over the imaginary net and be ready for replies. This style is an antidote to the waiter model. Its main feature for students is that it encourages you to use your voice in different ways. A real trap is to develop a habit of becoming so absorbed with individuals that your teacher-talk is never made public. If you spend the whole time going round whispering to students you actually have little presence in the classroom. Bring down the noise level so that you can talk across the room and be heard encouraging students publicly.

Snake charmer

This is a style which some teachers see as an ideal. You appear to be playing exactly the right kind of music and students come out of their baskets, do their work and go back again for the night, having tidied up. Although this is a stereotype, your aim is to generate a balance of responsibility and cooperation such that you do not actually need to discipline your class. The snake charmer happens when the tasks are so engaging, the students so motivated and the teacher is so in control that they can relax. Naturally, you need to find your own interpretation of this generalized stereotype. There are many other roles you can find yourself playing, from 'secondhand crockery seller', 'pleading vicar,' to 'screaming maniac' or 'pest control officer'. Invent your own, and recognize the comic side of teaching if it helps to get an impossible job back in proportion.

Lion tamer by default

Student teacher Mark had a difficult session with his class one Tuesday afternoon early in his practice. By Thursday he had decided that it was vital to concentrate on discipline or the children would play him up. Consequently, he was standing no nonsense at the start of the lesson and spoke to the children in short clipped commands, sounding businesslike and efficient. He wanted to explain how to draw a plan view of an alarm clock and this would be followed by the children attempting to draw their plan as they had been shown on the board. Rather aggressively he quietened the class and persisted in his aggressive control statements ('Sit still, Shane!' 'That means you!') until he had silence. A good feature was that he made sure, even through five or six attempts, that he got silence.

Unfortunately he did not lower the volume of his voice, be less aggressive or give praise to anyone. He still sounded annoyed and maintained the 'no nonsense' efficient tone of voice, stopping children as soon as they tried to speak. He told the children how to draw a 'top view' and a 'plan view', illustrating this on the board. No child was asked a question unless there was only one right answer which could be given. The lesson proceeded with threats, some silent working and further tickings off for not continuing to draw the plans well enough, inattention or being off-task.

Mark sat at the desk at the front of the room and children brought out their plans for him to check. A queue soon developed. So did the noise and children who were obscured by the queue began to flick pieces of paper. Mark began to lose his temper and imposed silence again. Everything depended on Mark's ability to keep students working and pounce on every deviation from his set plan.

Mark could have involved students at an early stage in devising criteria for what makes a good plan drawing, discussing this in small groups. Also, he could have made one of the criteria 'working well in a group' thereby emphasizing self-responsibility, awareness of others and learning to be polite enough to listen to the other children's ideas.

The skill of involving students

Students are not involved simply because you have decided that you will use an interactive whiteboard or make your lesson interactive. They need to pay attention to each other and to you. You may have tried out the script in Chapter 3 dealing with gaining attention – it is a well-known way to involve students, but one worth revisiting. It is a complete mystery why beginners are rigorous about gaining attention, then forget some of the basic ideas that they have learned about teaching. There is a self-check that you can try: observe your lesson and see if you are involving students by the frequency with which you use the words 'eyes', or 'look at'. Perhaps the most important word to use in gaining attention is 'eyes', as in 'I can't see all eyes', or 'Eyes this way' and its variants 'Looking and listening'. This is not enough in itself, because having got the students' attention, it is still necessary to move on and find other creative ways to involve them. When a trainee lesson starts to go adrift, you can almost place bets that the word *'eyes'* will have disappeared from the vocabulary. As if by magic, there are also fewer pauses and more attempts to control by shouting louder. Use an interactive whiteboard if you like, but direct attention too.

Given the chance to opt out, students would probably not listen to their classmates.

> They know if a student is about to answer, the rule is not to answer until everyone else is ready. I've trained my kids to wait if there is chatter and not give their reply. We have a 'no dis' rule. There is *no disrespect* when anyone is saying something. If any kids are not paying attention, I'm on 'em immediately! I click my fingers, or say quite loudly 'You might not *want* to listen, but you *will* listen because that's what we're here for.' (Primary teacher)

When this teacher clicks his fingers, he also points to the child. So long as this is not done too frequently (every idea in this book will fail if you overuse it) it has its advantages. Rather than finger-clicking, my personal method would be to say 'No disrespect', sharply and rapidly, then continue.

Involving students is a management task for you as a teacher. It is a minute-by-minute affair in which you are like the conductor of an orchestra, drawing out the appropriate melodies from your students. Success in this is influenced by:

- having rigorous codes about listening to other students and to you ('no dis');
- insisting on eye-contact from the outset when you teach a whole class;
- pointing to material you have generated and saying 'Look at . . .';
- checking to see that students are looking;
- involving students by naming them;
- having plenty of examples to look at, not just one;
- summarizing and verifying understanding;
- blocking irrelevant interruptions;
- asking questions;
- pursuing answers.

The skill of explaining

Why do some explanations confuse students and some clarify? If I told you that the *weffenplot* had three *dongblotchers* that needed to be aligned, you would be confused. The reason is you would have no idea in the first place what these words meant, no reference point from which to start. Good explanations have a logic to them and build on students' experience. There has to be a context, a sequence and a sense of meaning. Consequently, experienced teachers try to refer to previous experience and build from there. Explanations are effective if plenty of familiar examples are used, if they are are humorous if possible and memorable.

There are classic explanations that an experienced teacher uses, but they have not arisen by chance. Experience may tell you that pizzas or cakes are sliced to illustrate fractions, and the order of grid map references is remembered by the phrase 'Along the corridor and up the stairs'. There are helpful mnemonics such as 'i before e except after c' for spelling words such as 'receive'. Useful as these established reminders and analogies are, successful explaining involves much more. It is often a matter of judging when to break things down into smaller parts, when to stop explaining, when to summarize and when best to set students an activity. Too many ideas in one explanation can block students' understanding. Animals can be trained to count numbers up to a maximum of seven, and human beings can probably cope with a similar number of items in one go.

Two common faults when you begin teaching are explaining everything at great length or rushing your explanation. One reason why explaining at length can go drastically wrong is through the phenomenon of 'topic shift'. You begin by explaining one idea and just as that is being absorbed, shift the topic to something else so that students lose the initial thread. An example would be talking about reading a map, but shifting the topic to details about the scale of the map compared with other maps that you want to use. The new topic is certainly related to the old, but the explanation has ended at a much less useful point for map-reading. An obvious remedy is to shorten the explanation and stick to the point. When I first began teaching, the deputy head of the school took me aside and said: 'Make sure you keep all your explanations to 10 minutes at the most.' That advice might have been a little drastic, ignoring the value of interactive teaching, but it keeps an eye firmly on the boredom factor. Might it not be better, for example, to come back to the second half of your explanation after students have done a task which exemplifies the first part? There is something to be said for splitting up your explanation into manageable, 'bite-sized' chunks. A bite-sized chunk is between seven and 10 minutes.

Explanations will vary according to the complexity of the material that you want to teach and the context in which you explain it. Will you be explaining to five-year-olds or 11-year-olds? Will you be explaining the effects of static electricity or how to milk a goat? There is obviously a difference of level and expectation depending on the age of the students and their previous knowledge, the level of conceptual difficulty and the depth of understanding needed. Explanations of cause and effect permeate science teaching, while art or music require something more aesthetically driven.

There is a difference between asking a student to explain why a steel-built boat will float and to give the answer to finding 'two-fifths of 60'. If a teacher says 'Explain why the Vikings invaded Britain', this may be explanation as revision, logical conclusion or inspired guesswork. Some explanations are given to clear up misunderstandings, such as 'Can you explain again how to do this maths problem?', while others might concern new material, such as 'I'm going to explain how we use our school visit to find out about the Victorians'. Fortunately it is not necessary to know *all the time* whether your explanation concerns a concept, such as 'evaporation', a procedure, such as converting decimals to fractions, or a process, such as how a washing machine works.

Explanations work best if you can involve students by checking their understanding. This helps you to judge how well your explanation is going. You are more likely to hit the right level of explanation by picking up on the language that students use when they try to explain with you. You will find yourself clarifying words, stepping back from your prepared explanation and more easily adapting yourself to the situation. You are also more likely to summarize the explanation so far. This, in itself, can be done by you or it might be done through checking students' understanding; for example, by asking 'Who can tell me what we know about temperature so far?' Checking understanding can be a fine balancing act between listening and the need to press on. Peppered with examples, an explanation still has a logical sequence. Explanations are constructed, generally moving from simple examples to more complicated ones. A typical example of this would be learning to tell the time, where the sequence is first the hours, then half, quarter and minutes. After that, there is the 24-hour clock, digital and analogue displays. Remembering the earlier point about topic shift, most likely you will need to keep back part of your explanation.

A further dimension of explaining to consider is the extent to which you engage students' minds. Such phrases as 'Imagine this ammonite at the bottom of the sea', 'Imagine what it feels like to be lost in a forest' can trigger the imagination. So can problems engage the mind, such as: 'If I have 10 marbles and I give 20 percent to David, how many . . .', and stories such as: 'There once was a creaky house in a creaky town called . . .' or 'How to decorate using a feather'. A visual-aid accompanied by a story and questions is also a useful way to put your explanation across. Usually these entertaining parts of your explanation need to be followed up by clarifying the point that you are trying to make. Even though explanations often come at the start of a lesson, keep your mind on what you want to leave as an impression at the end. When you plan a lesson, it is well worth trying to think of an engaging idea, such as 'We'll find out what can happen to make sound disappear.'

Some explanations are rather abstract, such as trying to explain how electricity flows round a circuit. For example, you may use the analogy of ping-pong balls to represent electrons or water flowing along a stream to represent the direction in which energy flows. These mental images are useful so long as you make it clear that they are examples. If you use the analogy of an orange to explain that the Earth's crust is similar to the thickness of orange peel, you do not want students to believe there are enormous pips at the Earth's core. Most analogies fail when closely examined, so you will need to practise using them over time to see if they work. The examples and analogies you use are there to support explanations of *something*, and are rarely self-explanatory.

Analogies are often necessary to explain features of technology and science. There are fewer and fewer pieces of equipment these days that can be taken apart to see how they work. Many use microchips and computer circuitry, so what they do is far from obvious. If you take a mobile phone apart, there is little to show what is going on inside. The best you might manage is to draw a diagram using symbols and pictures to show text-messages travelling through space. Remember that you may be the only person who understands your analogy, so you will need to invite feedback from students to check that they have grasped the essentials.

The skill of questioning

Asking questions is the most effective way of verifying understanding. In school, students learn two unfortunate rules of questioning, even though these are assumptions on their part:

1 If an adult asks the same question again, then the answer I gave was wrong.
2 The teacher knows the answer.

Students try to make the teacher answer

Some students learn that 'If I wait long enough, the teacher will probably give the answer, or a few more clues'. A key skill to develop in questioning is to elicit answers without giving too much away about what you are looking for – you might do this by creating a habit such as 'Let's see how many answers we can get to this question', or 'I need lots of answers to this'. If you habitually invite numerous answers, you are more likely to encourage answers than if you stop at the first so-called correct answer. Instead of a 'hands-up' volunteering approach, there is a 'hands-down' one where you ask students by name to give their answer. You might begin by asking: 'Steven, see if you can remember the freezing point of water' (implied question). This can be a good opportunity to involve more students by asking 'Sarah, do you think that's true?', 'What do you think David?' In each case, the style of questioning is to invite students by name to involve them rather than have awkward pauses to fill. A further refinement is to ask a much more flexible question, such as: 'Steven, what's *your* explanation of how water freezes?', or 'Kirsty, what would stop water freezing?'

You probably know that 'closed' questions are those regarded as having only one possible answer. An example is to ask 'How many legs has a spider?', or 'Is it true that London is the capital city of England?' 'Open' questions are those to which there are several acceptable answers, such as 'Why does the weather change?' A useful tip here is to try to turn your questions into 'How?' and 'Why?' For example, as a teacher you might ask yourself 'Did the students understand my explanation?' Inevitably, the answer is going to be that some understood very well and some did not. An improvement is to ask yourself *'How* well did the students understand my explanation' or *'Why* might they not understand that part of my explanation?' 'How?' and 'Why?' are more likely to be tougher questions concerning the quality of teaching and learning. 'How?' questions imply 'To what extent?' and 'Why?' questions imply 'For what reasons?', often leading to deeper or more extensive answers. The importance of an apparently simple question is determined by its context. For example, you would need to know the context in which to understand Hamlet's line 'To be or not to be? That is the question.' There are more obvious classroom examples of context-dependent questions. A question such as 'What food did Frank eat?' could easily refer to a story that students are reading. However, the same question might actually refer to a detailed database about healthy eating. If it did, then considerable learning is involved in answering this question because the food data must be accessed first. Questions such as 'Which foods are salty?', 'Which foods are eaten raw?' or 'What percentage of the class prefers apples?' connect with other areas of learning. You may find yourself teaching mathematics and computing at the same time as discussing science. As an experienced teacher, you will devise questions that move learning forward, not just questions that check understanding and memory.

Although some questions have right answers, many do not. There is a questioning style called 'person-centred' which is different from the style of 'teacher-centred' questions. A 'person-centred' approach aims to ask 'What do *you* think, Kirsty?', 'Do *you* think that, Peter?' rather than 'What's the answer to . . .?' A teacher-centred question is: 'What is the main reason why the heat is lost from buildings in winter?'; the person-centred version of this is: 'Why do *you* think heat is lost from buildings, John?' Locked into a teacher-centred approach there is sometimes a tendency for teachers to ask a question and partly answer it, or pose it in such a way that only one correct answer will do. If you use a person-centred approach, things are different because initially there are no clues and sometimes no praise that might give the game away. Ask for as much information as you can without saying whether the answer is good, bad or something between the two.

If you want your questioning to grind to a halt, then give praise too early or keep on rephrasing the question. Sometimes praise can alienate students because every response is being judged by the praise it receives. 'Excellent answer, Charlene' sets a benchmark that others may not reach, so you may be better off collecting answers without implying value judgements along the way. What are you going to say if the answer is less than excellent? Praise, when you give it, is better given for effort and for having the courage to try an answer, as in 'Well done, Charlene, now we're getting some answers'. The error of rephrasing is where you ask a question, but before students have had a chance to answer, you rephrase it to make it clear (so you believe). If you rephrase or give too much help with answers, you may shift the topic. You think you have asked one question, but in reality you have asked three slightly different ones.

The traditional journalist's six questions are: who, when, where, what, why and how. The first three of these tend to produce closed questions which have limited answers. There are exceptions, but closed questions invite brief answers – 'right' and 'wrong', or 'yes' and 'no' responses. Examples are: 'When was the Battle of Hastings?' or 'Do you like raspberry jelly?' By comparison, what, how and why questions elicit much wider responses and are likely to form the wording of open questions. Suppose, for example, that there is a newsworthy item such as a fire in a theatre. Typically journalists might start by asking an eyewitness: 'What was the first thing you saw?', or 'Where were you when the fire started?', thereby generating information in chronological order. Once the starting point was established, the journalist would need to know where the fire broke out and when, when the alarm was raised, when the fire service arrived, who was there, who was missing or hurt, who escaped and so on. Most of this would be very straightforward fact-gathering with no speculation or deeper searching for issues. By contrast, a journalist might use the common device of asking: 'What was the theatre like before?', 'What is it like now?' and 'What might it be like in the future?'

Why and how questions might address issues such as why the fire started and how, how dangerous it was, how quickly it spread, how people reacted, and how it could have been prevented. The before–now–future inquiry is a useful format for encouraging debate, although it is less useful for mathematics and subjects where a different style will be needed.

Questioning sometimes goes wrong when a teacher asks fruitless questions. There are times when a teacher has to explain rather than question. Fruitless guessing seems to reinforce the fact that a student simply has no idea of the answer – it can be both intimidating for the student and unproductive for the teacher. Beginners need to ask themselves how much possibly can be guessed. A question such as 'What have you found out?' is clearly a useful one, but 'What is an ode?' supposes that the student already knows the answer. Guesswork can certainly involve a class, but if they really do not know the answers their guesses will confuse matters. In subjects such as science and mathematics, fruitless guesses could make it more difficult to arrive at the best answers. Ask yourself: can my students *really* be expected to guess the answers to this question? There are many questions of mindblowing complexity, such as 'Does God exist?' or 'Can the mind examine itself?' Other more mundane questions can still lead to varied and interesting answers.

Questioning is a skill because as a teacher you have to balance a range of options. These include who to ask and whether or not to follow up answers. Do you ask questions of many students so as to keep them involved? Do you pursue an answer with one student to find out more? Will you lose the rest of the class if you do this? Inevitably you will use a variety of questioning styles, sometimes following up, sometimes moving to another student and asking another question. This is guided by your objective in asking questions in the first place. What do you want to achieve? If you want to verify understanding, you will ask the same question several ways. If you want a wide range of answers, you will ask several different questions expecting several different answers.

You can encourage students to answer by waiting longer than you usually do. You may need to practise this by saying: 'I'm just waiting until we have nearly everybody with their hands up before I ask someone to answer.' It is also possible to make students think by reversing your question and answer. An example would be to ask: 'If the answer is blue, then what is the question?' A more sophisticated question would be: 'If the answer is: Sophie has more than Ellie, then what two questions could I have asked?' There are more than two questions possible and your aim might be to teach students to question an answer, or arrive at another answer. If you are a new teacher, take time to listen to answers because a class needs to feel confident that nobody will be made to feel stupid for answering incorrectly.

Questions for reflection

- What have you had to do already in a lesson to swerve away from your plans?
- What is your best way to calm down a restless class?
- How would you try to promote concentration as worth having?
- What sort of questions are more likely to involve students?
- What is most likely to prevent students answering questions?
- What makes an explanation a good one?
- How rapid is 'rapid intervention'?
- What contributes to the skill of working interactively with students?
- What value has verifying understanding through questioning?

Checklist summary

- React quickly, but speak slowly or you will sound agitated.
- Time to discuss work with individuals is always limited, but the occasional caring student check helps to keep them involved.
- A further dimension of explaining to consider is the extent to which you engage students' minds.
- The skill of reacting rapidly includes blocking interruptions if another student is speaking.
- Two common faults when you begin teaching are explaining everything at great length or rushing your explanation.

- If you split up your lesson into bite-sized chunks, you stand a better chance of avoiding topic shift. A bite-sized chunk is between seven and 10 minutes.
- A key skill to develop in questioning is to elicit answers without giving too much away about what you are looking for.
- Questioning sometimes goes wrong when a teacher asks fruitless questions.
- You can encourage students to answer by waiting longer than you usually do.

8

Coping with difficult students

Unsettling behaviour

Incidents engineered by difficult students are really 'isolated incidents', even if they recur within a few days. A curious feature of teaching is that if you lose control of your class one day, you can recover it the next. Behaviour management is second-to-second and minute-to-minute, so anyone can find themselves in and out of difficulties. Where an individual student is aggressive, defiant, insolent or disruptive this is also entertaining for the class. Whatever the isolated disruption happens to be, it must be handled so as to remain in control of yourself and therefore in control of the class. This was mentioned in Chapter 2, where it was suggested that you might say 'Ross needs some help here, so we will need to ignore him for a while. We all have work to do.' Your cool position here is to say to yourself 'Oh, I've seen all this before. It's just bad behaviour. If I pour fuel on this I'll have a bigger fire in no time. Back off.' Look bored and refer to the code of conduct, choices, decisions and sanctions already mentioned in previous chapters. Take a deep breath and put your emotions to one side, outwardly at least.

Approaches to coping with difficult students vary according to their age and circumstance, so you need some judgement about what to do for the best. A teacher of young children has this to say about a very difficult child. Whatever the age, the principle still applies.

> The most difficult child I ever taught was Oliver. At five years old he was so defiant that none of the usual things worked. He refused to do any work. I tried isolating him and I would say to the rest of the class 'Just ignore Oliver'. They were brilliant about it but Oliver would bang tables and make so much noise we couldn't actually do any work. I sent him out to the headteacher a few times and that didn't have any effect. All my best techniques failed and just made him worse. Do you know what worked in the end? TLC [tender loving care]. I got the class on side because they were astute enough to wonder why Oliver was getting so much attention when he misbehaved. I decided to ask them for ideas for what to do with Oliver, so I said: 'What do you like best when you're upset and angry, because we need to find what would be best for Oliver?' I ignored most of the replies until I got the one I wanted and I said 'Shall we try that cuddle idea of yours with Oliver and see if it works?' The class agreed. I would watch

Oliver and think 'Ah. He's about to throw a wobbly' and I would go over to him and give him lots of attention cuddles and praise before he went into a tantrum. Some mornings he would arrive in a bit of a state and I'd do my tender loving care bit by saying 'Oliver, would you like to help me get out these things? It's a really important job we can do together.' I had to be pretty keen-eyed to spot Oliver's mood, but it finally worked. (Year 1 class teacher)

TLC for older students is a bit more subtle:

You have to show difficult kids sympathy and understanding, but you can't always invade their personal space and get physically close. You have to let them know you understand and yet talk to them like adults. It's a question of their still having to do what they are asked, but plenty of praise when they don't expect it. Get in there before they realize, and try to make them feel important. (Year 6 teacher)

A few students, far from being cooperative, find themselves the centre of attention by creating serious confrontations. They swear at teachers, get into fights, refuse to do what they are asked, break equipment and disrupt teaching. Others are more the secret toilet-blockers and fire alarm practitioners, hoping not to be caught. A further group are those students who want to gang up with the class clown and 'torpedo' lessons for comic amusement. Difficult incidents with such students are unsettling for new teachers. When you are a beginner, you wrongly imagine that a difficult incident is a complete breakdown in your classroom control. In the heat of the moment the last thing you will feel like doing is responding positively. The scary feeling as a new teacher is not helped by anyone in the class who is determined to use every disruptive idea they can think of. The full repertoire of teacher-testing disruptions are thrown at you to see how you will fare. Will you lose your temper? Will the student get away with it? Clearly you have to do *something* rather than nothing.

Dan the disrupter

It is easy to forget that even the most difficult of students is looking for ways to be noticed and wanted by someone. In the midst of battles with teachers and unwillingness to cooperate, there is always some way out of a bad situation. By whatever means possible, the relationship between student and teacher has to be repaired and sustained. This is very tough, because disruptive and unlikeable students attract a great deal of negative comment. They are difficult to persuade, difficult to like (sometimes) and difficult to change. Even so, the way forward is still a positive repair of relationships through finding common ground and showing understanding but still directing attention for the good of the remaining students. For example, if Dan is late, a small gesture such as 'Good to see you, Dan' is more likely to win him over than 'Why are you late?' Saying 'Good to see you' makes it much harder for Dan to be objectionable to you because you have acknowledged him as a person. Tough TLC includes talking to Dan about himself, but also explaining to him about other people in the class. He needs to understand being sensitive about others if he wants them to care for him.

No quick fix exists for disruptive students. If one solution fails, all you can do is try another and another. Behaviour such as swearing, for example, is an outburst that challenges school behaviour policy, so you have a reference point. Stay calm and refer to the policy in place. If there is no obvious policy, invent one that has a series of stages. Some schools exclude a student for a day, others impose detentions, sanctions and inquisition by a senior teacher. As soon as you hear swearing you need to be fast enough to block any further words. Intervene like lightning and say: 'I'm not prepared to hear you swearing. I think you owe me an apology because that's not what this classroom is like.' Pause, stare and wait. Pause, stare and wait again. If necessary, wait again. The chance to apologize is far better than a student's immediate exit from the classroom. Most students will respond, but if they do not, you are likely to exclude them via a time out. Shrug your shoulders and try: 'I can see you are upset and angry, but this is no way to sort things out.' If there is an apology do thank them for it, but make it clear that the matter is not over yet. At some later point you will need to talk through the incident with the student, establishing what they might do instead of swearing, fighting or whatever the crime may be. Signal that you want to discuss this later (now if the situation permits). This is important to do because the student needs to learn alternative ways to cope with their outbursts. Badly-behaved students are not animals, but the way that some of them are handled can be a little like training a difficult horse.

> We've got this badly-behaved horse. Every time there's a new rider, he rears up and tosses his head to see what you'll do. If you don't react, he tries something else and then something else. After that he just gives up and lets you ride him. (Livery stable owner)

Dealing with the class clown

Any student whose behaviour is challenging soon attracts recruits to a small disruptive gang if you take no action. This is particularly true of the class clown. You will need to take action to isolate them because of what happens to the rest of the class if you do not. Clowns need a good audience, so you need to work hard to remove that luxury – once the audience has gone, there is not much of a payoff. Class clowns are difficult because they are often genuinely comic and can easily promote uncontrollable laughter. They have a strong influence in any class. This is such a destructive force that you may need to enlist the support of a colleague to take your class clown for time out elsewhere. Often, older children can develop a clown culture which is competitive between several students in the same class. Some of the advice given here does not fit an older class, so you will need to set your own agenda of serious work-related countermeasures in place. This may include having a laugh yourself, then making it clear that laugh-time is over. A sense of humour helps.

If you decide to isolate a class clown, you may sit them in another part of the room away from friends. Traditionally, this has always been at the front of the class, removed from the nearest classmates. Unfortunately this can mean that the clown turns round and continues to entertain from the front, so a better position (depending on room layout) can be to isolate the student at the side of the room. Wherever you choose, work hard at giving positive feedback to the clown about good choices and the work ethic. This can dispel an atmosphere of frivolous entertainment, bolster concentration and drive your lesson forward. Tell the isolated student: 'You'll work far better here and when you can prove that, I'll think about letting you choose where to sit.' This ensures that you explain the reason why the student has been isolated and leaves the door open for improvement.

> Josh is the class clown in Year 1. I said to the class, 'If anyone laughs when Josh is being silly, we'll be staying in at playtime.' Josh pouted, probably because he had been isolated psychologically. Nobody laughed and Josh settled down. I think it was because Josh didn't want to be the one responsible for keeping everyone else in. (Trainee teacher)

I would love to think that I could win with swift repartee and out-joke the class clown. You may fare better than me. I would prefer to say to the rest of the class 'Yes. I know he can be a laugh, but we've got too much work to do for that to continue.' Older students in Year 7 or 8 have a line in repartee and challenges that a beginner would find hard to match. Stick to what you know and avoid becoming embroiled in a comedy competition. Clowning is an attempt to hook you into taking the bait and provide opportunities for further joking. Some teachers are better than their students at repartee but this has all the high risk of a winners' and losers' game – brilliant for whoever wins, but an emotional downgrade for the loser. One can think of some very smart replies to the student who intends to continue clowning, but most of them would lead to suspension as a teacher. Drifting into sarcasm is not a solution either; a more acceptable remark might be:'If you want to be a clown, then join a circus. In this classroom we don't show off like that.' Remember that bullies often think what they do is for 'a laugh'.

Physical attacks

There is no end to the creativity of difficult children. They will hide under tables, steal pencils, and mutter insults when told to go back to their seat. There are differing levels of disruption, including hair-pulling and physical abuse, which can lead to fighting. The most serious physical incidents require that you resolve matters further up the chain of disciplinary responses agreed by the school. Many senior teachers or headteachers who have violent students sent to them do not take immediate action. They park a student outside their office to cool down. In a grave voice, stonefaced, they then begin their major speech culminating in consequences to fit the crime. I have seen this begin quietly and crescendo as the minutes tick by. When it is well done, with lots of awkward pauses and threats to involve parents, students are left in no doubt about the gravity of the situation. When you are more experienced, your admonishing and relentless 'grind-em-down' speech will trip off the tongue.

Bottom pinching the teacher

A Year 2 child has decided to pinch the new teacher's bottom. Unfortunately this *does* happen to teachers, but more often child-to-child. Engage with eye-contact, but do not stand close to the student. It is more effective to stand away and signal a lack of the usual social space between two people. Then say, as boldly as you can manage:

> Don't you *ever* do that again. You have the right not to be touched and I respect that right. I wouldn't do that to you and I don't expect you to do it to anyone else. I wouldn't pinch you, hit you or push you around. Everybody has the right not to be touched if they don't want to be. You do, they do and so do I. Do you understand that? [*Pause*] Do you understand that? [*Pause*] What are you going to do about it? [*Pause*].

Follow this up by taking the student aside to endure a more awkward moment, such as being questioned ('How do you feel about this?' or 'How do you think they/I feel?'), which can lead you to unravel the emotional side of the incident.

Some teachers milk situations for so long that the children finally surrender, worn down by the lengthy uncomfortable inquisition. Your style may be slightly different. Making children feel very uncomfortable while they are being ticked off can be a necessary part of the process if you do not want physical abuse to become a feature of your classroom. One of the best ways to do this is to pause and look as if you have finished, then suddenly return to your major speech adding difficult questions and spelling out unpleasant consequences. Eventually, your aim is to end on a note of self-responsibility, praising the student's capability to act in a responsible adult way. Life is imperfect, so a child will agree to behave well, even shake hands, then seconds later thump the living daylights out of the next victim.

If you impose sanctions, examine the certainty of the consequences you have set up. Small punishments reinforce your certainties, stepped in severity from five minutes loss of time to 10 minutes, 30 minutes, detention, more detentions, parents contacted and eventually exclusion. There is nothing so ineffectual as several threats followed by a massive loss of time or privilege. The stronger the system you have for following agreed codes of conduct, the easier it is to deal with difficult incidents. You do not have to stop to think what to do if there are agreed rules and routines, known levels of disruptive behaviour and consequences that are understood.

Avoid shouting

Faced with an angry student, some beginners remain convinced they should shout. All this tends to do is to inflame matters and is rarely as effective as keeping your cool. No challenging student ever cooperated with a teacher who was nose-to-nose with them, shouting and sometimes spitting in their face. In some rare instances it has provoked the student to spit back. You may feel angry and upset, but it is never inevitable that you should be personally upset by outrageous behaviour. Your power is not necessarily at stake, even if you think it is. You are a professional handler of difficult students in the customer services department of a classroom. The difference is that the customer is not always right.

If you shout, you are forgetting everything written in Chapter 6 about the way children mirror what you do. You may want to strangle a child as an example to the others, but that is your inner fantasy. Think of the mirror, and think of what you want to achieve apart from venting your feelings. One technique that works is to begin by shouting back as if you are just as angry, but calm yourself down in seconds. By doing this, you hope to hook the student into watching your identical body language and voice change. Some angry students will mirror you and calm down.

Difficult students quickly invite a sharp ticking off. Finding a script or two for this is sometimes hard for trainees to develop because they worry that they might start something that escalates bad behaviour. Many beginners do not realize that they can make a strongly negative comment so long as they are regarded already as a positive teacher. Beginners often shy away from ticking off students who deserve it. They probably fear the consequences, and this is understandable because they do not want a confrontation that they cannot handle. Meanwhile, they praise students because they believe that it works. Every teacher they meet probably tells them that this is a good thing to do and far more effective than criticism. This is true, but if you are positive, then a negative comment does not cause resentment. The balance of positive and negative comments needs to be about five positives to one negative. If you test this for yourself, you may be surprised to find that your world does not fall apart when you tell students off. If a student is abusive to another and punches them, you can relaunch your usual ticking-off speech, adding a few different phrases.

Refer to rights

'You punched and gave a kick, ignoring our class rules about behaviour. You have the right not to be punched and so does everyone else. I wouldn't do that to you and I don't expect you to do it either. What you did is *not* acceptable behaviour in our classroom and it is *not* acceptable behaviour anywhere else either. We do not

(Continued)

hurt anyone in this classroom. It is bad behaviour and there is no excuse you can give for it. I'm telling you this because everybody has the right to be treated well. You do, they do and so do I. I need you to think about how you can change things and help to make this class a better place to be. Do you understand? [*Pause*] You can do better than this. You can do well and you can succeed. I'm giving you a few minutes to think about this and I'll ask you again what you're going to do to sort it out.'

There is no guarantee that a disruptive and aggressive child will give you an answer to a question like 'Do you understand?' After all, you are ticking them off. You will notice that examples in this chapter are long ones, rather than a couple of one-line ripostes. This is quite different from a brusque warning ('Last warning, Liam!'). The intention is to give no idea of when you are going to stop. Other teachers may give a ticking off in tones of gravitas, raising guilt. Whenever you launch into a lengthy remonstration, all the culprit wants to know is when you are going to finish. This is a good feature of a ticking off. Sometimes the words matter less than the uncomfortable minute or two delivered with an appropriate tone of voice.

'Don't do that!'

Whenever I see a sign that says 'Don't touch', I am sorely tempted to rebel. If you say to some students 'Don't do that!', the temptation for them to disobey is irresistible. For most of the time, the word 'don't' is counterproductive because it has no message about what to do instead. The exception to advice about avoiding the word might be 'Don't you *ever* do that again', which is followed by enough detail in its moral outrage to blur the negative 'don't'. An occasional negative is forgivable, and it has real impact if used rarely. 'Don't' is a shortcut to stop what is happening.

Positive comments, suggesting what to do, are meant to focus on the behaviour but not negatively on the person. An example is: 'Darren, I like you, but I do *not* like what you're doing right now. Try again Darren, and remember what's expected in this classroom. It really isn't difficult and you're quite capable.' As a general item in the speech you might want to end with: 'You need to make more skilful decisions.' This leaves the student with a better sense of self-responsibility.

Some classroom behaviour is plainly so unacceptable that you will short-circuit and shout '*Stop!*' Shouting once every six months can have a desired devastating shock effect (she never shouts, so it *must* be serious). Hitting, kicking and swearing are outside the agreed code of conduct for the classroom, so a shout to stop the student is in order. It has been recommended already that you have a speech ready so you can drone your 'not acceptable behaviour' speech to death. When you do this, block any interruptions that your difficult student may try to make, and remember to keep a physically safe distance. Discourage other children from joining in with a 'Liam! I'm talking to Mark, thank you', otherwise you will have two conflicts on your hands. A great deal of your success lies in putting off the moment when you will stop speaking, even if other students drift off mentally. Teachers bore students to death with restatements of rules, codes of conduct, responsibility and adulthood. Eventually they have worn down difficult children and topped this by telling them that they need to talk about this later. Again? Yes, again. Then again, finishing with 'What are you going to do about it?', possibly adding 'I think you owe the whole class an apology'.

The idea of apologizing to the entire class is not one I personally would enforce, but mentioning it as an idea can emphasize the common framework for behaviour. Beginners sometimes forget that a major speech leaves a psychological negative after-effect. It is important after a speech to return students to their work. In the case of individuals, the usual phrase is 'I need you to . . .' followed by whatever the task is to be. There is no point elaborating on the crime and then forgetting about work. Emphasizing the task again allows you to lower your voice, pick on a totally innocent student somewhere near to you and quietly praise them for working hard. The psychological message is 'I can be tough on bad behaviour and positive to someone else about working well'.

Do do this

In complete contrast to the 'don't' words, there are things worth doing. So far, this chapter has tended to focus on difficult behaviour and some strategies for coping with it. Before this becomes cure rather than prevention, I want to emphasize the importance of ongoing feedback. You will find that the most difficult students resist work and ignore instructions. In my experience, if you sort out and clarify their understanding of the task, check they are able to do it and give feedback, many of their problems disappear. Positive feedback is a definite 'do' for disruptive students. Assuming they know where the equipment is, understand the task and have started, they still need a measure of trust and praise. They will probably spin out the task and do very little unless you intervene very early and praise them at the stage that they have already reached. You can hardly say 'Well done, you put the date at the top', but you can and should say 'Well done. I can see that you have already managed the first part . . .' You need to describe specifics in this first part to make this work and never to underestimate the frequency with which they need positive feedback, for example: 'Well done. You've already made a good start finding out what the Romans did to find water. Now you can get ready to say why the Romans built arches instead of solid walls on their aqueducts.'

Plan for difficult students – they may have low self-esteem regarding academic tasks, so the struggle is uphill. You do not want to insult them, but you do need to prevent disruption by making sure that:

- the task is achievable and they understand what to do;
- it is sufficiently open-ended to keep them going;
- you already know what you might praise, however small;
- you give encouraging feedback before they expect it (a theme already discussed in this book).

The curriculum is fixed only in its outline. The way you achieve a programme of study is much more flexible than you can imagine. Some teachers can make peeling onions seem attractive, yet others are the kiss of death to creative ideas. If you plan for enough variety in activities, at least you can say 'Well done' to your difficult students. There will always be something they managed to do.

Blocking difficult students physically

Blocking a student physically is a technique that isolates them for a few minutes. After you have firmly stated what you need Ben, the offending student, to do, turn your back and stand in front of him. Keep your back close to Ben to block out his view of classmates. Find any excuse you can to talk positively to the rest of the class. Talk for a couple of minutes, encouraging the class to work, discussing a learning problem or giving a reminder about what they are trying to achieve. Blocking with your back gives the offender time to cool off, but isolates them. It also refocuses the attention of the class on work so that other students are not tempted to join in and copy challenging behaviour. You may be able to praise the difficult student if they next settle to their work, although it is a good idea to restrict this to a 'Thank you' rather than specific praise. Standing close to a student with your back to them is uncomfortable for them because it is not what people usually do, so you put them in a position where returning to a task feels better than staring at your back. Blocking is not a perfect strategy because students are not always sitting where you want them to be, nor do they respond in exactly the same ways. Move the student to a place where blocking is easier, if that helps for future lessons.

It is never possible to predict exactly how a very difficult student will respond. One of the strongest responses, apart from remaining calm, is to persist with politeness because you build up an unassailable model of personal behaviour. You can do this and block a student at the same time. The rest of the class can see you are being reasonable. Many teachers put up with grunts and 'Yeh what?' from their students, choosing to ignore impoliteness in their classroom. You may decide that ignoring grunts is a better bet than challenging them, but you have every right not to accept these farm noises. There is a difference between grunts and mutterings as a student goes back to their task and an impolite response to their name being called. The way to challenge this is simplicity itself. All you need say is: 'Excuse me. I haven't spoken to you impolitely.' Pause and wait. If nothing positive comes from this, then repeat those words *exactly*. If that does not work, ask the student to try speaking again (see also Chapter 4 on being hooked by the bait). When you remain polite, you retain power in the classroom. There are truly difficult students who hardly know the meaning of politeness, but model politeness to them anyway. It will be far more effective in the long run. If there is a golden rule to be extracted from previous chapters, especially if students swear and insult, it is: never underestimate the power of describing what you want, and offering to discuss the disruptive behaviour later.

The 'disappointment routine'

Angry and difficult students are usually light years away from imposing self-discipline. You have another strategy left which is your 'disappointment routine'. In this, you find ways to act out that you are disappointed and feel let down. This routine has a long history in schools and the classic version, now the butt of comedy, is: 'You've let the school down, you've let me down and, worst of all, you've let yourself down.' Less clichéd versions are to say:

> Simon, I'm really disappointed by what you've done. I expected more from you.
> I'm *so* disappointed because I always thought of you as being responsible.
> I'm disappointed you've made the decision to misbehave, Ross. How could you make a better choice?
> You're very capable and I'm disappointed by what you've done today. You need some success so you can feel better about it.

I once saw a deputy headteacher call out to a student in the corridor. All he said was 'Not *you*, surely? I thought you were better than that' and the student became very tearful. The 'disappointment routine' is powerful, however briefly you signal it. Disappointment is also a key player when you bring back students from time out because they may still be resentful. Returning students to work requires a signal that the price has been paid and there are no grudges. You can say 'David, I was disappointed, but we can work on that now it's over. You're better than this and you can show me that. OK? Thanks David.' This is not a moment to force any comment from David. You are letting him know that he has a clean start now and no grudges are held against him.

The power of your 'disappointment routine' depends on plenty of positive behaviour modelling. Some teachers I have observed take politeness to extremes. There is so much 'please' and 'thank you' that my toes curl when I visit their classrooms. I am careful to stand up straight and take my hands out of my pockets in case I transgress their code of politeness. The positive side to all this is their students really *are* polite to one another. The teacher might drive students to kill each other with politeness, but it certainly gives them a platform for being disappointed when their students misbehave. The 'disappointment routine' has a strong emotional bite to it: maybe it is something to do with the parent and child relationship, trust and high expectations.

Students need to know that teachers disapprove, but if you use the disappointment routine, make sure that you do not pile on such disapproval that your students feel worthless. End on a positive note by saying what you want, such as the example suggesting that Ross finds a better choice to make. Spell out the alternatives and try to make them look like choices.

Leaving a way out

In the example that follows, there is something strangely addictive about doing things against a timer. Notice how the trainee gives the stubborn student a way out by deferring the deadline for putting shoes on.

> I had another run-in with my stubborn girl who refused to put her shoes back on during a carpet session. I announced to the class that I would give her three minutes to put her shoes back on and swiftly turned the sand timer over and carried on. A child piped up that she still hadn't put her shoes on after one minute. I said that I wasn't worried because I knew that I could trust the girl to put her shoes on by the time the sand ran out. The best bit was that she did! (Trainee teacher)

Blank refusal ('You can't make me!') has been mentioned previously in Chapter 5 concerning choices. Defiance, refusal and a good old sulk are close friends. Beginners find them frightening if they have no additional strategies to use. Defiance can be accompanied by swearing and smashing equipment if a student is angry. Clearly, you do need a strategy to handle this situation without overreacting. Some children, especially very young ones, can be taken over completely by their emotions. I once visited an infant school years ago, to be told by the headteacher: 'We can't go in my office because Carl is trashing it at the moment.' Carl was six years old and during my visit I never saw him come out of the room that he was busy smashing to bits. This was Carl's cooling off time, something necessary with very young children, although not always so dramatic.

A way out for Joe

Imagine you have had to reprimand a Year 6 student, Joe. In the absence of Joe's cooperation you have decided to say 'Joe, I'm not going to discuss this right now. We'll need to talk later if there's no change to how you behave.' You did this to let Joe cool off, but Joe needs to be left with a way out of his difficulty. His way out comes when you add 'Think about whether you *really* want that to happen. You're making the situation difficult when it really doesn't need to be. You don't really need to do that, Joe. You can carry on like this if you like, but it *will* result in making things worse. I'll come over and look at your work in a moment. Let's see if you can make a better decision.'

You have not closed the situation down with a 'see me later' directive. You have let Joe do some thinking for himself and hinted that there may be a change in consequences if he changes his behaviour. Tone of voice matters here, so try to end on a quieter, very serious tone of voice.

Walking away from a difficult student is very powerful. It avoids further argument and leaves the student wondering what to do next. Sometimes this is all you can do, indicating that you are too busy to talk any more and have better things to do. Probably your follow-up will be further discussion, a sanction such as a lost privilege or time lost. Beyond this are the next steps such as a trip to the headteacher or contacting parents. When students are very stubborn, they are best left with choices and deprived of a confrontation.

Behaviour plans and anger management

Up and down the country, students are on individual behaviour plans. Sometimes these include a record sheet with stickers and a comment from the teacher. For example, imagine that a boy in your class is frequently put on a behaviour plan. Whenever he is taken off his plan, he does something else so that he can go back on it. Why does he do this? He enjoys the attention that his plan gives him and feels more important doing his plan than just being part of a lower profile group. The cure for this is to suggest that the next plan is to memorize the plan and not have it marked and stickered. There is the promise of stickers for good work anyway.

First and foremost, a behaviour plan needs to be devised by the student as much as the teacher. A key feature of any good plan is to identify the undesirable behaviour and suggest an alternative. This is probably easier for a teacher to do than it is for a child, but resist as much as you can. A strategy that has some credibility is to help the student understand which behaviour is unacceptable, then run through as many options for alternative behaviour as possible until some decisions can be made. Rather like the strategy in Chapter 3, there is a 'when', an 'instead', and 'I will'. An example of the first part of this strategy is linked to emotionally-driven behaviour:

> When I feel I want to get a lot of attention I . . . [shout out, interrupt, laugh out loud].
> When I just feel bored and don't want to work I . . . [make stupid noises, throw things, stop other pupils working].
> When I don't want to join in I . . . [sit away from everyone else, sulk, refuse to do things].
> When I feel I am being bossed about I . . . [get stubborn and angry, shout out, knock things over].

Persuading students to identify unwanted behaviour is often difficult. In several of his lectures in Norfolk schools during the 1990s behaviour management consultant Bill Rogers suggested that the teacher asks the student's permission to demonstrate what the unwanted behaviour looks and sounds like. Most students will agree. The teacher then mimics the behaviour as closely as possible. Even if the student disagrees and says 'I don't do it like that!', the topic has been opened up. Unless there is some agreement about which behaviour is not acceptable, there can be no useful discussion about what to do instead. The aim in asking permission is to involve the student without creating resentment. Nobody wants to be mimicked without being asked first. Remembering to do this is part of the process. The second and third parts may look like this:

> Instead of [shouting, laughing] I will . . . [put my hand up and wait, see you after for help].
> Instead of [making stupid noises, stopping other students working] I will . . . [remember that other students need to work, so I need to try again].

The good 'I will' resolutions might also include practice sessions with a teacher. Again, some role-play can be helpful, depending on how cooperative the student is. With permission (never without) you might involve other members of the class in helping the disruptive student to put the plan into action. Plans are difficult to implement because they fly in the face of human nature, especially when a student is highly charged with emotion. The fact that a plan is on paper, possibly signed by both teacher and student, helps to clarify what is happening. There is no guarantee that the plan will work, but at least there is a plan.

It is a short step from this strategy to anger management. The most disruptive student behaviour tends to include anger leading to loss of self-control. If you dwell too much on the anger that you object to, you will not make progress with a student's anger management. As in the examples given so far, the real focus needs to be on how to behave when we feel angry, not how terrible you think it is to be angry. Anger management for students is likely to be the result of a carefully-agreed plan with plenty of emphasis on 'Instead I will . . .'. When you have established an anger-management plan, you will still need to intervene. If Darren is about to explode, you will need to shout 'Darren. Remember your plan!' Darren might put the brakes on his anger or he might not, but at least you were there to remind him.

A script for defusing anger between two students

BBC Four transmitted a documentary series in 2005 called *Être et Avoir*. One of these episodes was about life in a rural French primary school (*école primaire*) run by a teacher who was in the role of father, mentor, counsellor, communicator and guide to a wide age-range of students. Roughly following the subtitles, here is a translated transcription of a counselling discussion with two fighting nine-year-old boys, Olivier and Julien. The reason for including it here is that it represents a good example of how to unpick a problem without resorting directly to blame. Guilt is raised in both boys, but not as a means of damning them. The tone of voice used here is a gentle, yet probing, voice tone with a strong sense of caring.

Teacher:	You're the same age and roughly the same build. But why has there to be a winner? Is there any sense in that? Is it important for you? [*Long pause*] I know this has been building up for a number of days. You get on well sometimes and at other times, not at all. There must be reasons. Shall we talk about that? [*Pause*] What are the reasons? Olivier, what is your problem with Julien? You can tell him in front of me. [*Even longer pause*]
Olivier:	It's when he insults me. [*The teacher repeats this and turns to Julien*]
Teacher:	You see Julien, the words you use hurt him and he can only fight back physically because that's very important to him. It's very easy to insult someone, very easy to use the words that you do. Words, nice or nasty, are easy to say but you can hurt people. Perhaps Olivier feels hurt by the words you use, Julien? [*Pause*] Can we put a stop to all that, eh? And another thing. You're in a class with younger children and you're not giving them a very good example to follow. You both should be showing them that we can all get along as friends and work together. From now on we need to find a more peaceful atmosphere. We need to work in that direction Julien. Do you feel you can do it? [*Another long pause*]
Julien:	Yes.

Counselling students of any age is a skilful and sensitive area, but problems between students need to be teased out and dealt with without falling into the trap of apportioning blame. It would be so easy for the dispute between these two boys to continue as a stalemate of 'He started it!' and 'No I didn't!' Instead, the teacher's final reference is to the ethos of the classroom, responsibilities and implied codes of adult behaviour. To repeat: a golden rule here is to refer to the behaviour and not the person.

Practising, not excusing

Challenging students do not naturally arrive with developed social skills. You are unlikely to be running a finishing school, but students still need to understand that they have basic manners to observe. Bad behaviour cannot be excused because there is a group responsibility to consider other people in the class, whether or not they are friends. For some students, wrapped up in themselves, there will be an uphill struggle to convince them of this. What will you need to practise with your class?

- Basic manners.
- Coming into and going out of the classroom.
- Giving out and returning equipment and books.
- Sharing equipment.
- Putting things back where they belong.
- Putting chairs under the tables/desks.
- Returning pens.
- A polite 'go back to your seats' routine, when the students are on a carpeted area or gathered round for a demonstration.
- Behaviour during tasks.
- Picking litter off the floor.

Part of your role as a teacher is to teach these social skills as well as your subject knowledge. For some difficult students you start at square one because they are so used to fending for themselves. Teaching difficult students how the classroom is run is not a matter of nagging them. You may find yourself doing that, but you need to practise specific skills instead. Putting chairs under tables is an easy one if the students know that they will not leave the room until this is done. More difficult are the day-to-day polite dealings when students are not exactly friendly with each other. Your antidote to this is to take out the personal element. For example, Shane is taught to be polite to Liam who is sharing the scissors. He needs to be responsible for being polite, not because it is Liam, but because 'we do not excuse impoliteness in this classroom'. Similarly, 'We pick up litter, whoever dropped it, because that is how we leave a room' (students will always claim not to be the one who dropped the litter). When you refer to behaviour as a collective responsibility, not a personal one, you save yourself arguments. Practising good manners would be patronizing, but stopping students in their tracks and reminding them of whole-class responsibilities is not.

Some students remain difficult throughout their entire school career and beyond. If there are days when you seem to be nailing a jelly to a wall, that is exactly how it often is. Difficult and challenging students may improve, but you cannot change what is happening in their personal lives. A great deal is outside your control and theirs, but you have a strong influence on them and you can make a difference.

Questions for reflection

- What teacher-talk is effective for giving a ticking off?
- How do you keep the rest of the class on-side?
- What is your way of dealing with the class clown?
- What place have class rules and codes of conduct in dealing with disruption?
- Can you dislike a student's behaviour and still like them?

- How would you design a behaviour plan?
- What other ways are there to leave a student a way out of a situation?

Checklist summary

- Tender loving care (TLC) is irresistible.
- 'I'm not prepared to hear you swearing. I think you owe me an apology because that's not what this classroom is like.' Pause, stare and wait.
- 'I can see you are upset and angry, but this is no way to sort things out.'
- Behaviour management is second-to-second and minute-to-minute, so anyone can find themselves in and out of difficulties.
- When you remain polite, you retain power in the classroom.
- 'Excuse me. I haven't spoken to you impolitely.' Pause and wait. If nothing positive comes from this, then repeat those words exactly. 'Excuse me. I haven't spoken to you impolitely.'
- Emphasizing the task again allows you to pick on a totally innocent student and praise them for working hard. The psychological message is: 'I can be tough on bad behaviour and immediately positive about working well.'
- No teacher ever succeeded by setting a worthless task or one that could not be understood.
- For most of the time, the word 'don't' is counterproductive because it carries no message about what to do instead.

9   Survival and practical organization

Survival? What the heck's that about? Frankly it's a question of having a good laugh about your teaching. You could get seriously wound up when they misbehave or you could decide not to. I guess for me a better attitude is to think: 'Whatever will they try next?' See each day like you're trying to win at Trivial Pursuit, or a chess game or something! They're dopes when they misbehave, and you have all the cards stacked in your favour but they don't know that. I think what's kept me going is finding what they do is actually funny rather than a battle. They're so difficult sometimes, but I'm the world's best spotter of chewing-gum aficionados and competitive farmyard noise merchants, bum pinchers and sulkers. I think you should love them and laugh at yourself because they're at a stage in life where they have to find stupid new ways to feel important. Teaching is a job, not a religious crusade. If you're humourless about it, you'll end up stressed to death. Find these crazy kids funny and you'll like them, which means in the end they'll like you, won't they?

(Primary science teacher)

A life of blunt pencils

As a new teacher you want to do well. You might even believe that the job can be achieved to perfection, but it has only ever a few glimpses of that. Most of the time you will be trying to ensure that there are fewer blunt pencils, missing pieces of equipment and late students. These concerns are the boring trivia of life in a classroom. You will spend hours saying things such as: 'If you've made a mess you need to clear it up, even if we run into extra time.' You will set up routines that you can rely on because they make for an easier life. Belief in yourself is central to success, but belief that perfection is achievable is not the best motivator for anyone. In my career one phrase in particular has kept me going. When I was a trainee teacher I read in an education book: 'Few people teach so well at the age of 60 as they did when they were 30.' I found this to be utter rubbish, but I have kept it in the back of my mind as a reminder that it just might be more motivating to teach better each year, not worse. In the depths of a cold January morning, faced with a bunch of difficult students, all we have left is our professionalism to keep us going.

Survival depends on stepping back and recognizing that we are there to do our job. There are thousands of schools full of thousands of children. Naturally enough you will be emotionally involved with teaching and agonize about what you want to do for particular students who need your help. Would it not be better to remember that there will always be thousands of schools and thousands of children demanding a teacher's attention? You are at your very best when the top of your list of priorities is professionalism. This does not rule out caring for your students – in fact, professionalism is caring for all students regardless of their ability, social status, creed, ethnicity, and behaviour. Not caring breeds cynicism. It is impossible to create a warm and positive atmosphere in your classroom yet distance yourself like a cold fish. Professionalism is being able to be a warm-hearted, enthusiastic teacher and still end your day knowing that you have upheld notions of what you believe to be quality. This means you have been as even-handed in dealings as possible – and most important of all, have taught something worthwhile to your students.

Stress release and 'moan-bonding'

The job of teaching will always be overloaded with initiatives, some of which can be achieved and others that will cause frustration and stress. Staffroom relationships are rife with opportunities to 'moan-bond' with another colleague. Ever since I can remember, this activity has taken place in every school I have been in. Usually the headteacher is a reasonable target for any staff moan-bonding, alongside the government and whoever it was took someone's coffee mug without asking. Survival in teaching is helped by a small and insignificant amount of moan-bonding about colleagues and work, but not by very much more. Teaching has always been like this, even if you think there was once a glorious period of autonomy and freedom. Moan-bonding is enjoyable, but unfortunately it can breed negativity in staffrooms and, worse still, encourage the compulsive staffroom moaner. There is a thin line between moan-bonding and a frequent complainer who wants someone else to fix their problems. The moans of the complainer are out of all proportion to the problems and their effect can be very draining for anyone within earshot. It is as if moaners want to have their complaint validated because they see themselves as powerless victims of the unjust forces surrounding them. They are problem-*sufferers* who have yet to make the move to becoming problem-*solvers*. The only person likely to feel better after a 20-minute moan is the compulsive moaner.

I mention this because I have done my fair share of moaning, and have been quite unaware of the effect that it was having. Apparently, most of us moan about quite trivial things and the way this works is simplicity itself. Once we find a good staffroom listener the temptation is to offload excessively onto them, and there seems to be no stopping us. It is not that the day we have had has been totally devoid of positive things happening. Positive outcomes count far less in the stress stakes, so we tend to offload the negative items. In the middle of a good old moan, we need someone to say 'Yes, that's right', even if it is not, because we need our feelings to be validated. Understanding this process makes very little difference. One suggestion is to think in advance of something good that has happened before going home to offload. Or better still, why wait until then? Think of something before the end of the day.

Bad day, good day

For me, a bad day is one where the students have not learned very much, rather than one where they have been difficult and badly behaved. A good day is not just one when students have behaved very well. That might be part of it, but a good day is where I have sensed that the students have really achieved something and so did I. A good day is one where the lesson objectives are very clear and the students respond well to them, a day when creativity and enthusiasm are present, my lesson is lively and students can hardly bear to stop working. A bad day is where behaviour management has had so much of my attention that it has almost become part of the curriculum. This may be why I wince when I hear teachers telling a class how well they are behaving instead of how well they are working. It is very easy to lose sight of your intentions and be sucked into a life of behaviour management, dishing out rewards and punishments for behaviour. Obviously there is a strong connection between behaving well and learning something worthwhile. The ultimate reward in teaching is to see progress, and that requires more than good management.

A bad day usually means that just too many things went wrong (probably three things in a short space of time). That perfectionist streak rises to the surface and minor incidents turn into major catastrophes. You may find this happening at any time, but especially when students flout agreed work habits and behaviour codes. For example, you might have established a ritual for leaving the room based on trust. Instead of a step-by-step approach that includes instructions to stand, put chairs under the tables then line up, you are able to say: 'We're ready to finish now.' As far as the class is concerned, this signals responsibility for several routine matters to be completed before leaving the room. You might have established already that anyone not completing these steps will be called back, and you expect your ritual to be followed. Even so, flouting the expected adult behaviour (punching another student on the way out, disturbing another class, leaving litter and untidy areas) can feel like failure sometimes. Fortunately, just because events feel like failure it does not mean they are.

Some teachers reframe their bad day by redescribing it more positively to themselves. Others use the strategy described in Chapter 3 – *Whenever* (the student's behaviour) . . . *instead of* (my current behaviour) . . . *I will* (give a different response). They have a strategy ready for next time. One teacher I knew kept a box of 'Thank you' cards sent to him by grateful students and their parents. He would read these again on a bad day to remind himself of his successes. Another just let the world turn for 48 hours while he was operating mostly on 'autopilot'. There are days when you will feel that you have lost the plot, but that is all the more reason to remember that you are teaching children, one of the least predictable species on the planet.

Some of your best lessons will fall on deaf ears and some of your worst still make connections for some students. It is impossible to tell exactly what part of your lesson will strike home without reading the signals that children give back and thoroughly verifying their understanding. Students construct their understanding and this takes time and frequent repetition in some cases. Better than being the best is to be professional, giving the best that you can, and reflecting on the outcome as being a construction block in a long process of building. The occasional buzz gained from high achievement, high grades and recognition is not to be denied. Setting high standards and ambitious targets is, after all, part of good teaching. Self-rating is not. The process of rating – comparing ourselves with real or imagined genius (how it *should* be) – is needlessly stressful.

Developing your best teaching habits

There are nine ingredients worth including to develop your best teaching habits. The list that follows is a synthesis of points made earlier in this book. Some of these are antidotes to drifting off mentally and aiming for nothing in particular. Others will remind you of what has been written about questioning techniques and the value of summaries:

- teach your class with a sense of urgency, or they will set the pace instead;
- involve them by continually directing their eyes, pointing to anything written, and verifying understanding;
- check they are looking, if that is what you want them to do. Scan and scan again to check this;
- learn the power of a pause, followed by lowering the volume of your voice;
- block attempts to interrupt you with well-meaning questions when you are trying to focus attention;
- develop a questioning technique that elicits numerous answers before placing any value on the responses;
- keep using short ongoing summaries because repetition helps learning;
- give students a quality target to aim for, especially during individual, paired or group tasks;
- give plenty of positive feedback to students about their work and effort.

Giving positive feedback when students are working is a skilful business because of the timing and judgements involved. You do not want to intrude on students when they are busy working or they might lose concentration. This means that the occasional short 'Well done!' as you pass by a desk can be more helpful than an interruption. One feedback example is a teacher who has a folded card for each student that they keep on their desk. On one side of the card is a face with a smile and on the other is a face with a downturned mouth. If the student needs help, they turn the miserable face out so it can be seen. The system is not foolproof but can be a useful way to let a teacher know about successes and problems.

Most students need a positive reminder about their previous learning. This is sometimes overlooked by newly-qualified teachers, but is a powerful means of hammering home ideas. Positive reinforcement of previous learning need not take more than a couple of minutes, and it sets the context for what follows. You might say 'You may remember last week when we did a lesson about isosceles triangles?' and follow this up with questions that remind the class. Half the class may have forgotten, but the positive reinforcement of their learning can trigger memory and develop understanding. Watch students leaving a classroom and you will see the shutters of the mind come down on what you just taught. Unless learning is reinforced it can be lost in the past, so any opportunity to reinforce it is well worth taking.

One of your best teaching habits is to let students hear their name in a positive context, not a negative one. Imagine what it is like for a student whose only contact with you is a negative one. They want to hear 'Liam, good that you're listening' rather than 'Liam, stop chattering'. Part of the problem that some children have is that they are not used to being treated like people in their own right. They are used to being told off and criticized on a daily basis, so the more you can include them in a positive way, the better the relationship with them is likely to be. You may draw your own conclusions from the following comments heard on teaching practice discussing the same boy in the same class, taught by two different trainees.

> 'He's a pain. He's lazy and I can't stand him.'
> 'He's badly behaved, but I really like him and he works quite well for me.'

The most difficult students are not going to improve by being nagged, punished and rated as failures. Punishment has a temporary effect in many instances. Separating bad behaviour from the person who is behaving badly is very hard to do, but necessary if progress and better relationships are to be maintained. When the difficult boy taught by the trainee who described him as 'a pain' was observed, he clearly knew how to wind her up. She soon had a furrowed brow and was increasingly negative ('Darren, stop that! Darren!') in most of her contact with him. The class teacher returned and quickly picked up on the situation, sat down beside Darren, beamed him a large smile and asked him politely and positively how he was getting on. Darren, of course, was fine when with a one-to-one style of teaching, but the lesson for the trainee remains. Continual nagging is not going to work with the Darrens of this world.

What is nagging really like?

Sometimes, teachers who nag their students are not really aware that it is nagging. They take the view that it is blindingly obvious that things need putting away, doing better and remembered next time. Something about the voice tone bites into the children's bones.

> *John,* you've left that *again!*
> If you put it back where it's *supposed* to go you won't even have *to look for it*, for good-
> ness sake!
> *How* many times have I said this?
> *How* many times do I have to tell you?
> If you just pay attention more you'll *learn* more, won't you?
> You're *late* again! How are you ever going to learn *anything*?

The student may have the behaviour, but the teacher has the nagging. Difficult though it is, you need to ignore the behaviour that you do not want and replace it with praise about what you do. A trick here is to talk about tasks as if they have *already* been done. Not every class will respond, of course, but most will. (The following remarks could be said sarcastically – which would cause them to fail – or with genuine warmth, which stands a better chance of succeeding.)

> [*Before something is put back*] I really appreciate that being put back. Well done!
> [*When John is not concentrating*] John, we really appreciate you concentrating. Well
> done!

There is a slim distinction between nagging and reminding, mostly depending on your tone of voice. You might be surprised to discover that many remarks that are genuinely warm can be misinterpreted as nagging and sarcasm by older students. Praise and reminders given with the wrong voice tone tend to sound insincere and sarcastic. Reminders often sound like nagging unless they are carefully phrased and refer to the class, rather than individuals ('We need to leave the room tidy'; 'there's still some equipment to return'). A nagging teacher is often resisted by students and is not a very good example. A better way is to make it clear what needs to be remembered and say things such as 'We can't go yet because there are things to be remembered about how this room is supposed to be.' At least this prompts students to think for themselves.

There are recurrent problems in schools that encourage nagging. Two of these are student lateness, and inappropriate chatter. In first schools, the late-ness involves parents because they deliver their children to the school door.

Where there are specialist rooms for teaching, it can involve students arriving late for lessons. Annoying though this is, it needs to be recorded rather than nagged. Many schools keep a record of lateness and follow this up, but the more you nag students for misdemeanours and lack of attention, the harder your job will become. A better way is to stick to the principle that 'taking action is better than no action'. This may take the form of writing down notes as if you seriously intend to follow them up later. Do this in front of the student and say nothing, as if a bomb has now been timed to go off at an unspecified time. For added effect the book can be coloured black, which is traditional for these reports. Records of lateness or making notes about a student's bad behaviour may need following up or ignoring, but the effect of recording them is rather mysterious. There is a hint of 'I'll see you later about this' or there may be possible involvement of the headteacher or parental contact. Fend off enquiries about what you will do. Just record or say 'We'll see'.

One example is of a teacher who has a system called 'Four times and you owe me'. Her students agree a penalty in advance for being late four times. It is remarkably effective, rather like the fixed penalty on a driving licence leading to a court appearance and total ban. Agreed penalties can be given without emotion and followed up so long as there is evidence written down. Some teachers would go further with older students and have a signed contract of compliance, although with very young children this would be meaningless.

Feeling important by behaving badly

> You see, he's an adorable child but he has another side. He'll be nice in class and beat up other kids in the playground. So I took him on one side and said to him: 'Is that how you get to feel important, bullying other kids?' He couldn't answer and I didn't expect him to. But the important bit was to say 'Do you think there might be another way to feel important?' Again, he wouldn't answer, but I think he might move his mind on this a bit. (Year 3 teacher)

A theme in this book has been that bad behaviour is most often a student's way of feeling important. This was explained by the French teacher in the previous chapter when sorting out differences between two boys. Insults make the perpetrator temporarily feel better, as does bullying and a variety of show-off behaviour patterns. The search for positive ways forward almost certainly means finding better ways to feel important, whether this is by being given responsibility or being made to feel part of an accepted group. If we could wave a magic wand over difficult students and make them feel important for behaving well, then we would. Unfortunately it is an uphill struggle to remain positive with some students, so a suggested variation here is a development of what has been said already about the strategy 'When . . . instead of . . . I will'. The last stage of this can be taken a step further so that it becomes 'I will find a better way to make the student feel important'. Such a development will stretch your creativity to the limit, finding important responsibilities and valuing the slightest shift towards cooperation. The idea is to substitute attention-seeking behaviour for behaviour resulting from being given importance.

Responsibility is not exactly something that all of your students will understand. It is an abstract concept and one that is learned by example. Few young children will understand that they have responsibilities as well as rights, and the demonstration of this will need frequent use of the word 'responsibility' (as a young boy I never understood what my parents meant *exactly* when they said 'Behave responsibly'). You will need to repeat phrases such as: 'You're responsible for keeping your hands and feet to yourself', 'You're responsible for checking that scissors are returned', 'You're responsible for looking after the thermometers for this science lesson.' Alongside other words such as 'concentration', 'self-discipline', 'adult', 'patience', 'consideration' and 'politeness' you can develop a vocabulary that borders on propaganda. You do not need to nag students, but they do need to hear that these words are a frequent part of your vocabulary. You need to demonstrate them.

How organizing the classroom affects behaviour

No two classrooms are ever set out exactly the same. The most impressive I ever saw was disabled Rosie's Year 5 classroom, which was organized so that she could cope with her wheelchair. Displays were done at weekends with the help of her husband. The quality of Rosie's teaching was legendary. 'Enabled' would be a better word to use than 'disabled'. There was space between tables for the wheelchair, and students were very good at reorganizing the class layout as Rosie wanted it to be. The reason that the layout worked was because the entire environment emphasized cooperation and tolerance between teacher and students. Chairs were kept under tables and students were careful not to block Rosie's path to their table. The classroom was fit for its purpose and reflected Rosie's teaching style. Rosie had one rule that was never even stated: 'Don't offer to carry anything or think about opening a door. I can do it faster than you can!' The message was that Rosie had organized her room to maximize cooperation. You do not need to be in a wheelchair to understand how the principle can work in any classroom. Simply explain it to your class. Talk incessantly about cooperation, sharing, trust and responsibility if you want your principles to sink in – demonstrate and reinforce with examples whenever you can.

Any arrangement of furniture and equipment that is practical and works is a reflection of what you want to achieve. Resources tend to dominate classrooms and there is something to be said for deciding whether to have them around the edges of the room (increased student movement) or in the centre (limited space). Day-to-day organization is actually influenced by a teacher's preferred style. In one classroom students frequently walk across the classroom to take a piece of equipment from its storage. In another, the teacher asks: 'Why are you out of your seat?'

The installation of interactive whiteboards has radically changed how a class-room functions, as have portable tablet computers and laptops. Students have had to be seated so that they can see a board, flipchart or projected image, so organizing space to the best advantage is constrained by architecture and practi-cal concerns about being able to see what is going on. Consequently, an impor-tant consideration when you use a whiteboard frequently is not so much the furniture but how you position yourself in relation to it. If you are right-handed, you will obscure work on the board for those students to the left of you; the reverse is true for left-handed teachers. This seems obvious enough, but you would be surprised how many times teachers are positioned so that their students struggle to see what they need to see. Position yourself and the students you teach so that everyone is involved and eye-contact is not difficult to sustain.

Further, workspace is organized according to the activity. Desks may be pushed back for drama class and pushed together for groupwork. Formal arrangements such as a 'U' shape or rows of desks may be needed for interactive whiteboard teaching. In each case, the layout is determined by what is to be achieved. In some science labs it is almost impossible to gain the attention of the class because of fixed seating. One example saw a teacher seating their entire class around the outside walls, each child facing the wall. This was like a mass punishment cell and there is no point in it whatsoever. Another teacher dispensed with desks and chairs for most of a day during a practical sculpture and painting project.

Questions you might ask yourself before organizing desks, tables and chairs include:

- Who is responsible for resources (students, staff, monitors)?
- How are shared resources made available?
- Does a resource box per table make sense or will it be sabotaged?
- How is equipment counted out and back?
- Where is equipment best stored (availability versus security)?
- How much equipment are students expected to provide themselves (varies from primary to secondary sectors in education)?

Whatever you decide, bear in mind that students find it unsettling to have furniture moved around at different times of the day unless they are used to it. This means that you need to allow for some disruption until desk and table arrangements are known by your students. In primary schools, students are used to moving into groups for literacy and numeracy, sometimes going to another classroom if there are set ability groups. When this happens, you will need to refocus attention (as previously described in this book). Movement anywhere around a classroom or school corridor is a golden opportunity for students to talk more loudly than you might want. Either you live with this, or lay down ground rules for movement.

Health and safety requirements and fire regulations permitting, you can organize space around a school to prevent students from running. This is usually a matter of placing room dividers and display units strategically to encourage walking. Long corridors tempt students to speed along them if they can because there is so little in the way to negotiate. The strategy of positioning items in corridors also applies to classroom layout. You will need an arrangement that is multi-purpose yet allows you to display work or create quiet workstation areas (if you have fixed computers). Primary school classrooms often have a reading corner, a time out corner and a wet area for paint and glue. All that can be said with any confidence is that there will be some dedicated areas in your classroom. These still need constant reappraisal because they can result in wasted space.

One successful approach to planning the use of space is employed by some military units. The last items to be established in a new building programme are the paths. Planners have been known to wait and see where personnel walk from one place to another, then put down a path. The same can be said of an efficient classroom. Design the layout as you think it will work, but observe it closely to see what students *actually* do within the allocated space and established routes. This does not so much apply to paths as to the availability of materials and their storage, use of desks, chairs and workspaces.

Conclusion

At the beginning of this book I emphasized the point that a class will behave well if the work that they are set is engaging, interesting, within their capabilities and worthwhile. Many behaviour problems arise when students are at a loose end and difficulties are compounded if this becomes a habit. There are aspects of a lesson that are nothing to do with the planning, such as the way you greet your class, the way you gain their attention, refocus, change the activity and end the lesson. What do you do, for example, if a student is not engaged in an activity? How do you sustain an activity if it is flagging? How do you involve reluctant students?

The answers to these questions do not just revolve around the work that the class is doing, but more importantly *how* they are doing it. The driving force behind good teaching is quality in whatever form it can be found. Good teaching, therefore, involves thinking about how well something is taught and learned, not just whether it was done. No plan or scheme in itself guarantees quality, but it is a mark of professionalism that you can produce work of a high standard. Quality in behaviour concerns quality in listening, quality in concentrating, paying attention to detail and checking for errors. These are not enough in themselves but they are there to serve quality in teaching and learning. Over-emphasizing behaviour management can mask the ultimate prize of quality and lead to dull tasks that keep students busy. Some teachers can talk of nothing else in the staffroom but difficult students. Others are more interested in teaching creatively, challenging students and making sure that their own career is interesting. If you are able to enthuse your students, motivate them and set work, that is a good start. It will take a little longer to understand how children think and learn. Maybe it will take longer still to understand why one student wants to work hard and another does not. The rest is down to a mixture of psychology and the management strategies needed to ensure that your students make progress.

A different checklist summary

Positive

- Position yourself and the students you teach so that everyone is involved and eye-contact is not difficult.

- Try to keep a sense of humour because, like it or not, children are crazily funny.

- Step back and remember you are a professional doing your job.

- Keep moan-bonding to a healthy minimum.

- Encourage self-responsibility in your students.

- Teach your class with a sense of urgency or they will set their own pace.

- Involve students by continually directing their eyes, pointing to things written and verifying understanding.

- Remember how valuable repetition can be for hammering home understanding.

Negative

- Don't block students' view of what is going on so that you cannot see.

- Don't be a miserable teacher with whom it's unrewarding to be.

- Don't try to be perfect because you will stress yourself in the process.

- Don't offload to the point where you drain your colleagues with your moaning.

- Don't make your students rely on you to be told about every aspect of their behaviour.

- Don't get sloppy and let the class determine how slowly they work.

- Don't just speak to the back wall and forget to look at the whole class.

- Don't just rely on saying something once.

- Give students a quality target to aim for.
- Don't just think that doing a task will be enough to ensure quality.

- Give plenty of positive feedback to students about their work and efforts.
- Don't forget to give praise and feedback to students about their work.

- Understand the difference between reminding and nagging.
- Don't nag students. Remind them instead.

- Sound warm and sincere in your praise.
- Don't sound sarcastic and insincere.

- Try to find ways to make students feel important.
- Don't make students feel insignificant.

- Take action, rather than not doing so.
- Don't ignore bad behaviour.

Bibliography

Ayres, H. and Gray, F. (1998) *Classroom Management. A Practical Approach for Primary and Secondary Teachers*. London: David Fulton.

Barnes, R. (1999) *Positive Teaching, Positive Learning*. London: Routledge.

Berne, E. (1968) *Games People Play: The Psychology of Human Relationships*. London: Penguin Books.

Cooper, P., Drummond, M.J., Hart, S., Lovey, J. and McLaughton, C. (eds) (2000) *Positive Alternatives to Exclusion*. London: Routledge.

Corrie, L. (2001) *Investigating Troublesome Classroom Behaviour*. London: Routledge Falmer.

Docking, J. (1996) *Managing Behaviour in the Primary School* (2nd edn). London: David Fulton.

Douglas, J. (1992) *Behaviour Problems in Young Children*. London: Routledge.

Hayden, T. (2003) *Class, Management and Learning*. London: Routledge Falmer.

Laslett, R. and Smith, C. (1992) *Effective Classroom Management: A Teacher's Guide* (2nd edn). London: Routledge.

McManus, M. (1989) *Troublesome Behaviour in the Classroom: A Teacher's Survival Guide*. London: Routledge.

McNamara, S. and Moreton, G. (1995) *Changing Behaviour: Teaching Children with Emotional and Behavioural Difficulties in Primary and Secondary Classrooms*. London: David Fulton.

Merrett, F. (1993) *Encouragement Works Best: Positive Approaches to Classroom Management*. London: David Fulton.

Miller, A. (2003) *Teachers, Parents and Classroom Behaviour: A Psychosocial Approach*. Milton Keynes: Open University Press.

Porter, L. (2003) *Young Children's Behaviour*. London: Paul Chapman Publishing.

Putnam, J. and Burke, J.B. (1992) *Organising and Managing Classroom Learning Communities*. New York: McGraw-Hill.

Robertson, J. (1996) *Effective Classroom Control* (3rd edn). London: Hodder & Stoughton.

Roffey, S. and O'Reirdan, T. (2001) *Young Children and Classroom Behaviour*. London: David Fulton.

Rogers, B. (1997) *Cracking the Hard Class: Strategies for Managing the Harder Than Average Class*. London: Paul Chapman Publishing.

Rogers, B. (2002) *Classroom Behaviour: A Practical Guide to Effective Teaching, Behaviour Management and Colleague Support.* London: Paul Chapman Publishing.

Rogers, B. (2003) *Effective Supply Teaching: Behaviour Management, Classroom Discipline and Colleague Support.* London: Paul Chapman Publishing.

Sharp, S., Thompson, D. and Arora, T. (2002) *Bullying: Effective Strategies for Long-term Change.* London: Routledge Falmer.

Sutherland, M. and Sutherland, C. (2004) *The Behaviour Management Toolkit.* London: Hodder Education.

Watkins, C. (2000) *Managing Classroom Behaviour: From Research to Diagnosis.* London: Institute of Education Publications.

Watkins, C. and Wanger, C. (2000) *Improving School Behaviour.* London: Paul Chapman Publishing.

Weistein, R. (2004) *Strategies That Work.* London: Paul Chapman Publishing.

Wragg, E.C. (1993a) *Class Management.* London: Routledge.

Wragg, E.C. (1993b) *Primary Teaching Skills.* London: Routledge.

Wragg, E.C. (2005) 'Question forum for NQTs', *Times Educational Supplement.*

Index